FALLING TERRORISM
AND RISING CONFLICTS

FALLING TERRORISM
AND RISING CONFLICTS

THE AFGHAN "CONTRIBUTION"
TO POLARIZATION AND CONFRONTATION
IN WEST AND SOUTH ASIA

HOOMAN PEIMANI

Westport, Connecticut
London

Library of Congress Cataloging-in-Publication Data

Peimani, Hooman, 1957–
    Falling terrorism and rising conflicts: the Afghan "Contribution" to
    polarization and confrontation in West and South Asia / Hooman Peimani.
       p.   cm.
    Includes bibliographical references and index.
    ISBN 0–275–97857–5 (alk. paper)
    1. Afghanistan—History—2001– 2. War on Terrorism, 2001–
    3. World politics—1989– 4. Terrorism— I. Title: Afghan "Contribution"
    to polarization and confrontation in West and South Asia. II. Title.
    DS371.4.P45 2003
    958.104'6—dc21   2003048221

British Library Cataloguing in Publication Data is available.

Library of Congress Catalog Card Number: 2003048221
ISBN: 0–275–97857–5

First published in 2003

Greenwood Press, 88 Post Road West, Westport, CT 06881
An imprint of Greenwood Publishing Group, Inc.
www.greenwood.com

Printed in the United States of America

The paper used in this book complies with the
Permanent Paper Standard issued by the National
Information Standards Organization (Z39.48–1984).

10 9 8 7 6 5 4 3 2 1

To my son Justin

Contents

Introduction

After years of devastating civil war, Afghanistan has entered an era that could potentially bring about peace and stability for the Afghans. Confined to about 10 percent of the country in the north for over three years, in late 2001 the advancement of the anti-Taliban Northern Alliance forces in different directions after weeks of American military operation suddenly changed the political landscape in Afghanistan. The Taliban regime's fall in November 2001 and the subsequent creation of an interim government ended over two decades of devastating civil war in Afghanistan and created grounds for optimism about the country's future stability both in Afghanistan, the main victim of the war, and in its neighboring countries. In one form or another, the latter have all suffered from the long-term instability in Afghanistan. In the absence of a civil war, the new political environment has a prerequisite of stability, a necessity for any type of economic development badly needed in Afghanistan. The sudden change in the political reality opened a new and hopefully peaceful and more prosperous era in the history of this war-torn country. However, it also set the ground for a new round of rivalry in South and West Asia geared to economic gains, political influence, and security considerations.[1] All those countries that have taken sides with the United States explicitly or implicitly over certain objectives, namely the removal of the Taliban and ensuring the stability of Afghanistan, have found little incentive, if any at all, to continue their cooperation in the post–Taliban era. The removal of the Taliban regime from the political scene also removed their common cause over which those countries with different or opposite interests became united temporarily. In the post–Taliban era, all of them, including the United States, have pursued their national interests, which are not confined to fighting terrorism, in general, and fighting Afghanistan-based terrorist groups, in particular. Stemming from peculiar national-based political and economic needs and imperatives and/or from specific state-determined perceptions of threats, such interests are different or opposite in nature. For all practical purposes, in the post–Taliban era, the old pattern of rivalry and conflict has emerged between and among the regional powers and the United States over political influence, economic gains, and security considerations in South and West Asia.

If the current pattern of relations between and among certain regional states (China, Iran, India, Russia, and Pakistan) and a nonregional state (the United States) continues, various factors will likely help develop such rivalry into confrontations between two camps or groupings of regional and nonregional powers. This will be a result of the polarization of South and West Asia in the post–Taliban era. Beside their long-term economic, political, and security implications for those regions, such confrontations will have a major impact on the shaping of the international system. Depending on the specifics of the international situation in the near future, the regional realities, and the priorities of the regional and nonregional powers with vested interest in those regions, those confrontations may take various forms. Regardless of their forms, the geographical, economic, political, military, and social links to certain regions and countries of the regional and global powers involved in such confrontations will make the latter's impact felt way beyond South and West Asia. This is owing to the international significance of China, Iran, India, Russia, Pakistan, and the United States for different reasons. In particular, their significance lies in their having certain characteristics, including their possession of about two-thirds of the discovered oil and natural gas resources located in their countries (Iran and Russia) or in their regions, namely the Persian Gulf and the Caspian Sea.[2] They also include their large and/or growing markets (China, Iran, India, and the United States). Finally, they are significant for their nuclear capabilities of different strength (China, India, Russia, Pakistan, and the United States).

As a former superpower with a global claim, the result of such confrontations will be of particular importance for Russia. Depending on its nature, it could help Russia address its numerous deficiencies, and thus function as a major factor in paving the way for its reemergence as a fully-fledged global power. Alternatively, it could further weaken Russia politically, economically, and militarily and therefore consolidate its current status as a regional power with a formidable nuclear capability in the process of erosion. In the absence of a strong and vibrant economy and its inability to project its power far beyond its borders in a significant scale, that capability is not a strong enough factor to make Russia a global power with its corresponding political influence.

Apart from its immediate impact on Afghanistan-based terrorist organizations, the war against the remnants of al-Qaeda and the Taliban in Afghanistan will reinforce certain regional trends. This will be the case regardless of its length and the various forms it may take over time. In particular, that war will gradually set the stage for rivalry between two major camps or groupings consisting of Iran, India, and Russia enjoying a degree of support from China and of the United States and Pakistan, which will pursue opposite objectives. As a result, the major long-term impact of the anti-terrorist war in Afghanistan will not be on Afghanistan itself, but on the two regions between the Mediterranean Sea and the Pacific Ocean in which the two camps have long-term interests. For their aforementioned significance, the future inevitable political developments in South and West Asia will have major effects on the shaping and the stability of the international system and on international peace and security.

The existing cooperation between the United States and a number of countries in West and South Asia aimed at the elimination of the Afghan-based terrorist groups is at best short term. For different immediate or short-term objectives, China, Russia, India, Pakistan, and certain Persian Gulf (e.g., Saudi Arabia) and Central Asian (e.g., Uzbekistan) countries have explicitly joined the American-led coalition operating in Afghanistan, in one form or another. While not a declared member of the coalition, certain factors made Iran its implicit member for awhile. They include its suffering at the hands of the Afghan-based terrorist groups and international drug-traffickers, its hostility toward the Taliban, and its backing of the only anti-Taliban armed group, the Northern Alliance (now known as the United Front), since the day of its inception. Thus, Iran contributed to the coalition by facilitating the fall of the Taliban through the Northern Alliance, as Iran, along with Russia, provided it with weapons and other types of assistance. Iran also backed the process leading to the creation of the interim government of Hamid Karzai before, during, and after the Bonn Conference of December 2001. As well, it helped the holding of the June 2002 Loya Jirga (Afghan elder and tribal leader assembly), which reelected Hamid Karzai as president for an eighteen-month period. By providing humanitarian assistance, Iran has since supported the Karzai government and committed itself to providing it with $550 million to be spent on reconstruction efforts.

The anti-terrorist campaign in Afghanistan has created an opportunity for the "coalition" members to achieve certain objectives apart from uprooting Afghanistan-based terrorist groups. For some, it has provided a legitimate pretext to suppress their internal opposition groups (e.g., China, Russia, and Uzbekistan) or to seek their regional objectives (e.g., India and Pakistan). For the Americans, their war on terrorism has opened opportunities for achieving certain strategic objectives, including expanding and consolidating their political, economic, and military presence in South and West Asia. The latter will put them on a course of conflict with many regional powers and states in those regions in addition to Russia. They are those whose national interests will be endangered by the American government's pursuit of its strategic objectives.

All the mentioned regional states and the United States have long-term objectives in South and West Asia. They go far beyond the campaign against the Afghan-based terrorist groups. No wonder if the Taliban's fall and the ongoing government-making process in Afghanistan, which will likely take at least a few years if everything goes well, have already set grounds for conflicts among them. The reason lies in the fact that the nature of the future Afghan government and its policies toward its neighboring countries will have major implications for their national and regional interests of various natures.

The state of relations between and among these regional and nonregional countries will gradually push them toward forming explicit or implicit camps or groupings to deal with the emerging political and military environment in South and West Asia caused by the recent developments in Afghanistan. Such camps will be created for short-term or long-term objectives as determined by their interests and the changing regional and international situation. For China, Iran, India, and Russia, concern about a rapid expansion of American political and economic influence and military presence in those regions either directly or via Pakistan will create a strong objective to prevent such a scenario altogether. Their perception of a long-term security threat will justify their collaboration. This will be notwithstanding their history of rivalry over issues such as the export of Caspian oil and gaining political influence in the southern CIS countries and of their disagreement over the division of the Caspian Sea among its littoral countries (Iran and Russia). Extensive and friendly relations among Iran, India, and Russia and the absence of major sources of conflict among them will facilitate their cooperation. Sharing many of their concerns, China will be a de facto member of this camp whose "membership" is facilitated by its peaceful ties with the other three states and its extensive economic relations with Iran and Russia. However, its history of conflict and rivalry with India, its grievances about Russia's treatment of China in the past, as well as its efforts to turn itself into a global power will likely make its full membership in the camp rather unlikely. Having lost its protégé (Taliban) and concerned about the growing influence of Iran, India, and Russia in Afghanistan and Central Asia, Pakistan will find common grounds to continue its cooperation with the United States, a country sharing its concerns for its own reasons. The two states began cooperating in the aftermath of the September 11 terrorist attacks on the United States. Their cooperation has taken the form of a formal alliance.

However, the American-Pakistani camp will not last for a long time. It will be fragile in nature as the Pakistanis will not likely find the Americans ideal partners for certain historical reasons and also for appreciating the fact that the American long-term objectives in South and West Asia will run against many of those of Pakistan. Pakistan's "traditional" suspicion about the United States has stemmed from its uneasy relations with that country since its independence in 1947. Based on their half-century of bilateral relations and on trends and tendencies in international affairs, the Pakistanis appreciate the strong American interest in extensive ties with their archenemy, India. Regardless of whether such ties could be forged at all in the foreseeable future, its possibility makes the Pakistanis uncertain about the commitment of the Americans to Pakistan, which could lead to their "sacrifice" in favor of India. As well, the Pakistanis are aware of the possibility of a future rapprochement between the United States and Iran, a rival neighbor and, in cases, an enemy of Pakistan. Added to other factors, the mentioned concerns and suspicions will likely weaken Pakistan's incentives to remain in the American camp. Being a dissatisfied regional power, its well-established and more reliable ties with China, another dissatisfied regional power, will further weaken those incentives.

Having ties with both camps, Saudi Arabia and Uzbekistan, like many other Persian Gulf and Central Asian countries, will likely try to maximize their gains out of the rivalry between the two camps by tilting or threatening to tilt toward one camp or another. If the current trends in Saudi relations with Iran and the United States continue, the Saudis will likely expand ties with Iran, India, and Russia as well as China in certain areas such as regional cooperation and trade. That will be a result of the geographical realities and long-term considerations based on certain trends in the Persian Gulf and the Middle East requiring cooperation and friendly ties with those countries, despite Saudi Arabia's interests in friendly ties with the United States. The inevitable future replacement of the current religious Iranian regime with a secular one will most probably create stronger incentives for collaboration and extensive ties with Iran, and by default with its camp, both among the Persian Gulf (e.g., Saudi Arabia) and the Central Asian countries (e.g., Uzbekistan). As revealed in many recent polls conducted by the Iranian government itself, the widespread dissatisfaction with the current regime also reflected in student protests all over Iran in late 2002 will make a change of regime a realistic scenario in the foreseeable future.

In its development of the main argument, chapter 2 deals with the significance of Afghanistan for the regional and nonregional powers. In this regard, after providing general information about the country, it offers a brief account of major factors determining the policy of certain regional powers toward Afghanistan in the contemporary era. As well, such factors will likely form their policies in the foreseeable future. The beginning point is the 1978 pro-Soviet coup as it shaped the pace of events in the following two decades and contributed to the formation of the current political, economic, and social situation. As for major regional and nonregional powers, the focus is on China, Iran, India, Pakistan, Russia, and the United States for the significant role that they have played or for their potential role in influencing the pace of events in Afghanistan. In its approach to the formation of groupings among them, this chapter elaborates on how and why their interests collided or coincided in that country prior to the fall of the Taliban.

Chapter 3 deals with the overall situation in post–Taliban Afghanistan. It analyzes the major trends and tendencies of political, economic, and military/security nature with major implications for the country itself and also for certain influential countries in its proximity capable of affecting its pace of events. In this regard, this chapter explains why the main regional and nonregional states with an interest in Afghanistan are concerned about and/or seek to influence its ongoing political and military/security developments. It also provides an account on the main objectives of those regional states, which, in one way or another, have taken sides with the United States in its "war on terrorism." Moreover, major objectives of the latter in Afghanistan are given an elaboration.

Chapter 4 focuses on the factors contributing to the gradual polarization of South and West Asia and the formation of two camps or groupings there. In this context, as the main catalyst, the impact of American growing influence in Central Asia, the Caucasus, Afghanistan, and Pakistan on the expansion of dissatisfaction among the regional powers is given special attention. Moreover, those factors eroding the commitment of the regional states to their "anti-terrorist alliance" with the United States are identified.

Chapter 5 offers a summary of major findings. In the light of such findings, it identifies possible scenarios under which the two groupings in formation could find themselves on a collision course. Moreover, the short- and long-term impacts of such groupings on regional and international settings are discussed. Attention is given to the parameters, which will weaken Pakistan's commitment to its alliance with the United States over time. Finally, this chapter elaborates on the circumstances under which the two camps could disintegrate.

NOTES

1. Throughout this book, unless otherwise stated, South Asia includes India and Pakistan while West Asia contains the countries of Central Asia and the Caucasus, Iran, and Afghanistan.

2. The Caspian Sea has five littoral countries (Iran, Russia, Azerbaijan, Kazakhstan, and Turkmenistan). However, all references to the Caspian Sea region or Caspian countries exclude the first two countries, unless otherwise stated.

2

Afghanistan and Regional and Nonregional Powers

GENERAL INFORMATION ON AFGHANISTAN

Geographical Facts

Afghanistan is a landlocked country located in West Asia. It borders three Central Asian countries of Tajikistan, Turkmenistan, and Uzbekistan to the north, Pakistan to the south and to the east, China to the east, and Iran to the west. Afghanistan has an area of 647,500 square kilometers. It has long land borders with Iran (936 km), Pakistan (2,430 km), and its three Central Asian neighbors of Tajikistan (1,206 km), Turkmenistan (744 km), and Uzbekistan (137 km), while having a short land border with China (76 km). Among its major cities, Kabul, the capital city, and Jalalabad are located in the eastern part of the country, while Herat and Zaranj are in the west, Kondoz and Mazar-i-Sharif are in the north, and Kandehar (Qandehar) is in the south.

Population

The population of Afghanistan was estimated at 23,294,000 in 2002.[1] This figure does not include the Afghans residing in Iran and Pakistan. Over the last two decades, the Afghan population residing in the country has decreased significantly as a result of the Soviet invasion of Afghanistan and its subsequent civil war, which lasted on and off until the Taliban's fall in November 2001. The unstable situation forced millions of Afghans to flee their country to settle as refugees in Iran and Pakistan. This pattern of population movement has persisted in the post–Taliban era as a result of the continued instability in Afghanistan, which makes the voluntary repatriation of the refugees extremely difficult. As stated by Iranian Minister of Interior Abdulvahed Moussavi Lari, 2.3 million Afghans were still in Iran in August 2002 despite the repatriation of over 100,000 before that month.[2] Political uncertainty and lawlessness, on the one hand, and a lack of viable economic opportunities, on the other, have ensured a very low rate of return to Afghanistan and a constant flow of Afghans into Iran. According to the Iranian Consul in Kabul, Ali Hoshyaripour, only 116,000 of Afghans residing in Iran left for Afghanistan between April and August 2002, while the number of Afghans entering Iran legally or illegally during the same period exceeded them.[3] Factors including far inferior government-provided care available to refugees have resulted in the repatriation of a much larger number of Afghans from Pakistan. In early September 2002, their number was estimated at 1,570,000 compared to 196,000 from Iran.[4] Late in 2002, there were still hundreds of thousands of Afghans in Pakistan despite an extensive repatriation program right after the Taliban's fall. Of those who have been repatriated to Afghanistan from Pakistan, many were expected to return despite the less than desirable situation for them in that county. The absence of basic infrastructure, employment, and an expected cold winter were among the major contributing factors.[5]

Afghanistan's estimated population growth rate is 2.5 percent for the period 2001–2016.[6] In 2003, the estimated crude birth rate is 48 births per 1,000 population, while the estimated crude death rate is 21 deaths per 1,000 population.[7]

The Afghan population is very young as evident in the following 2003 estimated breakdown based on age groups: 1–14 years (43.7 percent), 15–64 years (53.5 percent), and over 65 years (2.8 percent).[8] In the absence of reliable estimates, if the current trend continues, the Afghan population will be even younger by 2015.

Afghanistan's population is not ethnically homogenous. It consists of four major ethnic groups, namely Tajiks, Hazara, Pashtuns, and Uzbeks. The Pashtuns form the single largest ethnic group accounting for about 38 percent of the population, while Tajiks, Hazara, Uzbek, and others (e.g., Turkmen, Baloch, Kazakh, and Kyrgyz) constitute 25 percent, 19 percent, 6 percent, and 12 percent, respectively.[9]

Afghanistan is not an urbanized society. In the absence of a significant industrial sector, agriculture has become the main economic activity and the main source of employment and income. There are no statistics or reliable estimate on the numerical strength of the urban and rural dwellers. However, it is certain that Kabul, the capital city, is the largest urban area. Its population includes a very large community of internally dislocated people who have fled their regions because of insecurity and/or poor living standards.

Religion

Islam is the religion of the majority of the Afghans of whom most subscribe to the Sunni sect. The Shiite population mainly, but not exclusively, corresponding to the Hazara ethnic group, constitutes at least 19 percent of the population, while non-Muslims (Zoroastrians, Sikhs, and Hindus) account for about 1 percent of the population.[10]

Economy

Afghanistan has a devastated economy reflected in its very small GDP estimated at $18.39 billion in 2001 based on estimated GDP per capita of $820 and an estimated population of 23,473,000.[11] In the pre–civil war era, agriculture was the dominant sector, while the country lacked a modern and adequate infrastructure. The efforts of the pro-Soviet regime in the 1980s to establish and expand industry, to modernize and expand agriculture, and to address infrastructural deficiencies had only a limited success. Factors responsible for this failure included its practical lack of control over many parts of the country controlled by its armed opponents, its lack of popular legitimacy, its limited resources, and frequent interruptions in its projects because of the ongoing civil war. During the fourteen-year war (1978–1992) against the pro-Soviet Kabul regime and the Soviet troops, most of its limited achievements were destroyed along with most of the previously created agricultural, industrial, and infrastructural facilities.

In the absence of a fully-functional central government with a clear development plan, the continuation of the civil war after the toppling of the Kabul regime in 1992 destroyed most of the remaining farmland, light industry, and infrastructure. The civil war forced massive displacement of the population of the affected areas to safer areas inside the country and to the neighboring countries.

As a result, post–Taliban Afghanistan simply lacks a functional economy of any significance. What is left is mainly an agrarian-based subsistence economy, which is not even capable of meeting the basic food requirements of the Afghans. Consequently, they survive on extensive foreign-donated food and other basic requirements, which are in most cases inadequate to meet the growing needs of the impoverished population. According to an FAO/WFP crop and food supply assessment for 2002/2003 released in August 2002, Afghanistan would require at least 467,725 tons of food aid for about 6 million people dependent on food assistance despite a significant increase in cereal production thanks to improved precipitation.[12] Certain factors have prevented any major efforts to change the situation for the better. They include the continuation of the anti-Taliban/al-Qaeda war in part of the country, the resumption of local fighting between warlords in other parts, the weak central government, and a shortage of skilled personnel. They also include the absence of an adequate long-term foreign financial assistance package, an absolute necessity for the impoverished country lacking sufficient domestic resources. As a result, the existing overall situation is simply discouraging viable long-term economic activity.

RECENT HISTORY SINCE THE 1978 COUP

The roots of the current tragic situation in Afghanistan can be traced back to 1973. In that year, an intra-elite coup deposed Mohammad Zahir Shah, the Afghan king, who was in Italy at the time and who returned to Afghanistan only after the Taliban's fall. That event set the country on a gradual path of instability, which has continued to this date in one form or another. General Davood Khan, the coup leader, ended the monarchy and established an Afghan republic that lasted only until 1978 when a Soviet-backed military coup removed his short-lived political system.[13] That development laid grounds for the creation of an unstable and unpopular pro-Soviet regime characterized by constant internal fighting and by the inability to expand its power all over the country. During the first few years of the new regime, three presidents came to power through coups beginning with Nor-Mohammad Taraki who fell victim to a pro-Soviet palace coup bringing to power Hafizullah Amin only to be removed from the political scene by yet another pro-Soviet coup. Hence, President Amin lost power to Babrak Karmel when the Soviets invaded Afghanistan. He stayed in power until 1986 when Mascow replaced him with Mohammad Najibullah, the only president who did not come to power through a coup.

The 1978 coup provoked the rise of an armed anti-government movement backed by Afghanistan neighbors Iran and Pakistan. The weakness of the pro-Soviet political system, its internal conflicts, and the expansion of the armed opposition put it on the verge of collapse. To prevent the seemingly inevitable fall of its protégé, the Soviet government sent troops to Afghanistan in December 1979. The Kabul regime's weak military and security forces and its shaky social basis made it completely dependent on the Soviet forces. In an effort to expand the regime's control all over the country, their numbers rose to about 100,000 in the early 1980s. The direct massive involvement of the Soviet troops in fighting turned the civil war into an anti-Soviet war. Mobilized in different Mujahedin groups along ethnic and/or religious lines, the anti-Soviet armed Afghan groups received support in funds and arms from the United States as well as from Iran and Pakistan. The latter housed millions of Afghan refugees fleeing the devastating civil war, government persecution and/or poverty and hunger. Iran and Pakistan also provided shelters to the Mujahedin groups with positive attitudes toward them. By and large, Pakistan became the backer of the Pashtun Sunni groups while Iran became the supporter of mainly other ethnic groups, namely Sunni Tajiks and Uzbeks and the Shiite Hazara. Among other state supporters of the anti-Soviet movement, Saudi Arabia acted in a prominent manner by providing funds and by indoctrinating part of the movement with its fanatic version of Islam known as *Wahabbism*. To a limited extent, China also helped the movement through its backing of certain Mujahedin groups, mainly those few small leftist ones with a very limited role in the anti-Soviet campaign.

The Mujahedin war against the Soviet forces and the pro-Soviet Kabul government began in 1980 and lasted until June 1992. In the absence of a strong pro-regime military force, the Soviet forces became the defenders of the Kabul regime whose army operated mainly alongside them. For this reason, the Afghan civil war took the form of war against the Soviet forces until 1989 when they finally withdrew from Afghanistan, as a result of heavy casualties, high financial cost of operation, and the emerging dissatisfaction among the Soviet people. The Soviet withdrawal did not end the war, but changed its main focus now exclusively against the Kabul regime. The Soviets left it alone to defend itself, although it was unprepared. The weak regime became weaker in December 1991 when the collapse of the Soviet Union cut its only source of military and financial assistance on which it long survived. In June 1992, the Mujahedin forces captured Kabul and ended the Communist regime of President Najibullah who sought refuge in the United Nations compound where he stayed until 1996. In that year, the Taliban executed him as they captured Kabul and entered the compound forcibly.

The twelve-year war devastated the poor country. Massive aerial and land bombardments by Soviet forces and missile attacks by both sides of the conflict destroyed its inadequate infrastructure, its limited industry, and its underdeveloped agriculture, which was the country's main economic activity. The constant expansion and contraction of territories by the two parties to the conflict internally displaced millions of people, while forcing millions to seek refuge in Iran and Pakistan. At the end of the war, the country was devastated economically and could not even feed its own population.

The capture of Kabul and the establishment by the Mujahedin groups of an Islamic regime ended the civil war only for a short while. President Borhanedin Rabani, a Mujahedin leader, who formed a coalition government consisting of the leaders of major Mujahedin groups, failed to overcome the differences among the coalition members. That failure made him unable to create a functional central government and to consolidate its power all over the country. Consequently, conflict among the Mujahedin groups over their share of government led to the resumption of civil war late in 1992 and it lasted until the Taliban's fall in November 2001.

Without any exception, all the Mujahedin groups contributed to the initiation of a new round of civil war by seeking to get the upper hand in the new Afghan government. However, a major obstacle to the formation of a coalition government representing all Afghan ethnic groups was the Pashtun Mujahedin. The single largest ethnic group, the Pashtuns, who had traditionally ruled over the country did not want to accept a power-sharing arrangement leaving them with anything less than the complete domination of the political system. That scenario was unacceptable for other Mujahedin groups representing the rest of the Afghan ethnic groups who together accounted for the majority of the population. In this situation, the manipulation of such disagreements by regional powers worsened the conflicts between the two sides and finally led to the resumption of war, this time among the former allies. As will be discussed, Pakistan backed the Pashtun groups while Iran supported the others. In pursuit of their regional objectives, other countries in Afghanistan's proximity, mainly the Arab Persian Gulf countries, helped these groups to a more limited extent over time. The main characteristics of the new round of civil war was constant infighting between and among the Mujahedin groups over territories and frequent shift of loyalty resulting in the formation and breakup of many short-term alliances between and among rival groups over tactical objectives.

The new round of civil war further devastated Afghanistan and created hardship for the ordinary Afghans. Extensive human rights abuses committed by all the Mujahedin groups and the widespread lawlessness and chaos all over the country helped form a social constituency for the Taliban. The Pashtun group capitalized on the popular sense of frustration with the Mujahedin rule controlling different parts of the country as independent rulers. Their territories expanded and contracted frequently because of constant fighting between and among them. The result was the exposure of their respective people to constant violence and abuse of human rights both by retreating and conquering forces. Unsurprisingly, there was a growing desire for an end to the Mujahedin era among the Afghans. This popular demand for a strong central government in place of various Mujahedin governments coincided with the interests of certain countries also interested in a strong but docile Afghan government.

The rise of the Taliban in 1994 began a new dark era in the history of this war-torn country. Even though they came to the political scene with a promise to end the civil war, their emergence actually intensified it as they sought to subjugate all other rival groups in their bid to control the entire country. After two years of fighting with the rival Mujahedin groups, they captured Kabul in 1996 and pushed out the forces loyal to President Rabani backed mainly by non-Pashtun Mujahedin groups, first and foremost by the Tajik forces under Defense Minister Ahmadshah Massoud. By that time, over half the country was under Taliban control. The rest, that is, the territory to the north of Kabul extending to the Afghanistan border with its Central Asian neighbors and to the western provinces neighboring Iran, was controlled by the Tajik, Hazara, and Uzbek anti-Taliban Mujahedin groups. Stemming from their ethnic and political rivalry, their lack of a common strategy to fight the Taliban and their constant, fighting against each other made them vulnerable to the Taliban forces. Their efforts, jointly, in some occasions, or individually, in most cases, to recapture their lost territories in the south and the capital, Kabul, failed, but their military operations to that end contributed to the further destruction of their country.

In 1998, the Taliban's massive invasion of northern Afghanistan pushed them all out of most of their territories and confined them to about 10 percent of Afghanistan in the north, which was ethnically dominated by Uzbeks and Tajiks. Leaving with no other choice, the entrapped anti-Taliban forces gathered under a loose united front named the Northern Alliance backed by all anti-Taliban regional countries. Iran and Russia became the main supporters of the Alliance providing it with funds and supplies, including arms. Iran also became the safe haven for its leaders who established their headquarters there. As well, India, Tajikistan, and Uzbekistan supported the Alliance to a much lesser extent. Respectively, the last two countries backed the Afghan groups of their ethnic brethren, namely Tajiks and Uzbeks. The Northern Alliance's backbone was the Tajik forces under Commander Ahmadshah Massoud. He fought the Taliban since their emergence in 1994 despite his forces' weaker military capability, while others were not persistent in fighting against the Taliban and even, at points in time, showed a desire to compromise with them.

In the aftermath of the September 11 terrorist attacks on the United States, the Northern Alliance now reinforced by Iran and Russia and with assistance from the United States played the decisive role in the Taliban regime's fall. Excluding the southern and southeastern territories, dominated by Pashtun tribes, its forces recaptured most of the country's territories. Those tribes, with American assistance, rose against the Taliban regime a few weeks before its demise.

Taliban

In pursuit of its regional interests, the Pakistani government formed the Taliban in 1994.[14] Its main objective was to end the seemingly endless Afghan civil war and to unite Afghanistan under a pro-Pakistani central government. This became a necessity, as Pakistan's Pashtun protégé (*Hizb-i Islami*) seemed unable to dominate other Mujahedin groups equally incapable of ending the war in their favor. Against this background, certain factors created a social ground for the creation of the Taliban. Among them, one factor was the atrocities committed by the Mujahedin groups against each other and against the civilian population during the course of their fighting. Another one was the social and economic hardships created by the war and the frequent expansion and contraction of the territories under the rival groups. The Taliban capitalized on the frustrated people's desire for an end to the civil war, anarchy, uncertainty, and the Mujahedin rule over different parts of the country and for the creation of a single central government in full control of the entire country.[15]

Through different means and to a varying extent, over time Saudi Arabia, the United Arab Emirates (UAE), and the United States also made contributions to the Taliban's growth. Despite their differing backgrounds and their differences in a variety of issues, the major common objectives of all these states included their opposition to Iran for various reasons and to its growing influence in Afghanistan and Central Asia. Securing access to the newly independent Central Asian countries via a friendly territory was yet another common objective for the four states. For Pakistan and the United States, exporting Central Asia's oil and gas via Afghanistan and Pakistan was an additional objective.[16] However, the initial common interests of all these states did not last very long. The United States stopped supporting the Taliban regime after the 1998 bombing of two American embassies in Africa. The incident provoked an American missile attack on an al-Qaeda training camp in Afghanistan. It also caused the Americans to become hostile to the Taliban for its harboring of anti-American terrorist groups. In 2000, a suicide attack on an American warship (*USS Cole*) off the Yemeni coast further deteriorated American-Taliban relations. However, Saudi Arabia and the UAE continued their political and financial support of the Taliban until international pressure forced them to cut their ties with them in October 2001, a month before their fall.

Pakistan was the main supporter of the Taliban since its military intelligence, the Inter-Services Intelligence (ISI), formed the group in 1994. The Pakistanis were the main supplier of arms and the main provider of military training to the Taliban. They were also the major foreign beneficiaries of the group. Through its backing of anti-Iranian and anti-Indian armed extremist groups among other means, the Taliban helped the Pakistanis seek their regional objectives, including weakening Iran and India, Pakistan's main regional rival and its archenemy, respectively.

The Northern Alliance

The Northern Alliance (NA), known as the United Front in the post–Taliban era, has enjoyed to a varying extent and for a different period of time the backing of Iran, India, Russia, and the Central Asian countries excluding Turkmenistan. Their shared concerns have made all these countries united in their support of the NA. In the Taliban era, those concerns included their fear of the Taliban's spread of extremism directly or through its support of extremist and terrorist groups in their countries and in the neighboring regions. They were also concerned about the turning of Afghanistan into a safe haven and a training camp for extremist and terrorist groups with a hostile policy toward them. As well, the Taliban's direct involvement in international drug-trafficking with its devastating health, social, and security impact on many regional countries formed a strong incentive for a united action against the Taliban for whom narcotics became the main source of income and foreign currency. Finally, for Iran, India, and Russia, a shared concern was the growth of American and/or Pakistani influence in Central Asia through a Taliban-run Afghanistan facilitating the American and the Pakistani access to that region.

Drug Production and Trafficking

The production and trafficking of narcotics (opium, heroin, morphine, and hashish) have been a growing problem in Afghanistan over the last two decades. These activities became a major source of domestically-generated income and foreign currency for most of the Afghan Mujahedin groups fighting the Soviets and their puppet regime in Kabul in the 1980s and the early 1990s. The replacement of that regime with another one established by a coalition of Mujahedin groups in 1992 did not stop the narcotics "industry." The reason was the simple fact that the devastated country lacked any other significant industry, thanks to years of war and destruction. At the same time, there was no enthusiasm on the part of foreign countries, regional and nonregional alike, to help the Afghans create a viable economy when the latter lacked adequate domestic means to do so. In the absence of any other major source of income, foreign currency, and employment, drug production and trafficking became the only available type of worthy economic activity for many Afghans.

However, the emergence of the Taliban in 1994 and its subsequent control of about 90 percent of Afghanistan drastically changed both the local extent and the global significance of the narcotics industry. The Taliban allowed massive cultivation of opium poppy in their territory to create employment for poverty-stricken Afghan peasants, and also to generate revenue and foreign currency for their regime. That was a highly isolated regime recognized only by Pakistan, Saudi Arabia, and the UAE whose financial assistance for that regime was insufficient to cover the heavy cost of its war with its opponents, while meeting all the basic needs of the devastated Afghanistan. Encouraging opium cultivation aside, the Taliban regime gave a free hand to international drug-traffickers who established their drug-production "factories" in the Taliban-controlled areas. From there, they conducted their international smuggling operation to supply the markets of West Asia, the Middle East, the CIS countries, Europe, and to a lesser extent North America. Afghanistan under the Taliban became the largest global producer of opium, heroin, and morphine. In 1999, it set a world record by producing 4,600 tons of opium from which the other two narcotics are extracted.[17]

Besides its obvious global health hazards, drug-trafficking threatens the security of Iran, the southern CIS countries, and Russia, in particular. Drug-traffickers have resorted to military operations to secure a safe path to export narcotics from Afghanistan to Europe via Iran and the Central Asian countries. The bloody war between the regional security forces (Kyrgyzstan and Uzbekistan) and armed drug-traffickers in the Ferghana Valley in the summer of 2000, which resulted in hundreds of dead and wounded security personnel, is a well-known recent example of the destabilizing nature of their operation for Central Asia.[18] This region neighboring Afghanistan, the drug-producing country, and Russia, the country through which drugs are smuggled to Europe, is replacing Iran as the main drug route because of Iran's tough anti-drug policy. Besides the imposition of death penalty on traffickers, over 30,000 Iranian troops stationed along the fortified Iranian-Afghan border have been engaged in a two-decade-long war against the Afghan-based traffickers seeking to cross the border to supply the Iranian market and to access Europe via Iran's western neighbor, Turkey. The resulting heavy casualty on the Iranians during this period has demonstrated the depth of security threat of Afghanistan-based drug-trafficking to their country. According to the Iranian authorities, during the period 1982 to 1998, drug-traffickers killed 3,350 Iranian military and law enforcement personnel.[19] A few hundred more have since been killed.

Despite Iran's tough policy toward drug-traffickers, that country has kept its attractiveness for them for its large domestic market and also for its geographical position as a bridge between Afghanistan and Europe. However, over the last few years, a growing number of bloody skirmishes between drug-traffickers and Central Asian and Russian border troops along the Central Asian border with Afghanistan have indicated the growing security threat of Afghanistan-based drug-trafficking for the Central Asians. In the post-Taliban era, there has been an increase in the number of such incidents. As a recent example, in July 2002 the Russian border troop patrolling the Tajik-Afghanistan border engaged in a bloody fight with drug-traffickers and seized 215 kilos of heroin as they tried to cross the border.[20]

Placed under various UN sanctions for harboring terrorism, the highly isolated Taliban regime caved in to UN pressure and that of certain countries, including its neighbors, to stop poppy cultivation and to end narcotics production in 2000. Therefore, its reported production decreased from 4,600 tons in 1999 to about 200 tons in 2000, according to Ali Hashemi, commander of Iran's anti-narcotic force.[21] As the largest victim of drug-trafficking in the region with at least 2 million officially estimated drug-addicts, the Iranian government, which did not recognize the Taliban regime, offered that regime its help to transform Afghanistan's poppy fields into wheat fields. This policy was meant to create incentives for the Taliban regime then heavily dependent on foreign food aid to cooperate, and also to generate alternative employment opportunity for the Afghans cultivating opium. This crop-substitution policy did not change the situation drastically, because its effectiveness was confined to the extent that the Taliban was prepared to implement such a transformation. Its claims to have completely stopped poppy cultivation contradicted the UN assessment of the situation suggesting a 70 percent reduction in such cultivation at best, prior to its fall in November 2001. That assessment was confirmed by the continued production of opium, although on a much smaller scale (200 tons) in 2001.

THE SIGNIFICANCE OF AFGHANISTAN FOR THE POWERS IN THE REGION

For a variety of reasons, Afghanistan has been significant for various regional and nonregional countries over the last two decades. The poor, war-torn country with a rudimentary economy is not attractive to any of the regional and nonregional powers for economic purposes, although it has certain economic potential. The country is rich in precious stones and has mainly undeveloped natural gas resources, but the latter is not significant enough to turn it into a major global producer. The Afghans exported natural gas to the Soviet Union prior to the fall of the pro-Soviet regime in 1992. In the absence of strong economic incentives, many noneconomic factors have created stakes for certain regional and nonregional powers in Afghanistan, which vary from one to another. These factors have determined the overall policy of those powers toward Afghanistan and encouraged them to get themselves involved in that country directly or indirectly through proxies. As well, they have created grounds for their rivalry or collaboration, which have made a major contribution to political developments in Afghanistan. The continued existence of such interests will determine the pattern of involvement in that country of those powers in the future, while having a major impact on the future social, political, and economic development of Afghanistan.

Significance for China

China is a neighbor of Afghanistan with no ethnic or strong historical ties with that country. What has created a stake for the Chinese in Afghanistan has been its potential to become a source of threat to their stability and national security in two major ways. On the one hand, Afghanistan could turn into a hostile territory. On the other, its political developments could have a negative effect on China's stability.

China is concerned about Afghanistan turning into a hostile territory where regional or nonregional powers could establish military bases capable of endangering its national security. In such a case, Afghanistan would become a direct military threat to China, a scenario that the Chinese wish to avoid for certain reasons, apart from the obvious one. Being in the process of economic and social transition, China requires a long period of peace. For that matter, the Chinese have sought not to antagonize their ties with any country capable of posing a serious threat to their country. Within this context, the Chinese government has been especially concerned about its neighbors, namely India, Russia, and Afghanistan. The first two were the source of major security concerns for the Chinese between the 1950s and the 1980s. Their ties with the Russians began to improve in the last years of the Soviet Union when the Soviet government under President Mikhael Gorbachev was seeking a policy of easing tension and normalizing relations with all its traditional foes, including China.[22] Before that, the two countries experienced severe deterioration of relations, which began in the late 1950s. In the 1960s, their hostile relations took the extreme form of constant skirmishes along their common borders over territorial disputes provoked and aggravated by their ideological differences.[23] Since the fall of the Soviet Union, the two neighbors have sought to continue the process of normalizing relations as both require a long period of peace to address their various political, economic, and social problems, while having strong interests in trading with each other. The value of their annual trade has been in billions of dollars since the collapse of the Soviet Union. In 2001, it reached $8 billion.[24]

China and India have had uneasy relations since the 1950s. They fought a short border war in 1962, which further intensified their mistrust and hostility toward each other.[25] China occupied about 12,000 square kilometers of Indian territories before and during that war, according to the Indians.[26] As the loser of the war, India has looked at China not just as a source of threat, but also of embarrassment. The two countries have normalized their relations, which have been peaceful for the last four decades. However, their ties are far from cordial and friendly. Keeping its long-term interests in mind, the Chinese have tried to improve their ties with the Indians who have also showed an interest in that direction. In 2001–2002, the Chinese made an effort to expand diplomatic relations with the Indians as reflected in the official visits of a few high-ranking Chinese figures to India. Even though the two sides are still far from having extensive multi-dimensional relations, this mutual interest in improving ties reflects the two countries' concern about engaging themselves in hostile relations at the time when they have other potential or active enemies. Also, this indicates that both sides need peace and stability to address their numerous domestic problems, especially the economic ones, which have created obstacles to achieving their desired eminent international status.

As a neighbor of China, a stable, predictable, and friendly Afghanistan is essential for its national security. While the Chinese government needs to ensure that the country will not become a hostile territory housing anti-Chinese government groups, it is especially concerned about the long-term political direction of Afghanistan. For its numerous political, economic, security, and social problems, the militarily weak Afghanistan has not been, and will not be in a position to pose a serious threat to China for a predictably long time. However, the shifting of its government to a state hostile to China and its making available its territory to that state's enemy could pose a serious security threat to China. For this reason, the Chinese have been keeping an eye on political developments in Afghanistan for the last few decades. Without a doubt, the sudden shift in the political direction of that country in the late 1970s reflected in the establishment of a pro–Soviet regime through a military coup and its subsequent occupation by the Soviet troops created a major security concern for the Chinese. On hostile terms with the Soviet Union, China suddenly found itself surrounded almost completely by enemies. The massive presence of Soviet troops in Afghanistan completed their presence along China's long northern and western borders at the time when Indian troops and the pro–Soviet Vietnamese military were stationed along most of its southern borders. To break its encirclement, China became one of the supporters of the Afghan Mujahedin groups fighting the Soviets.

The Soviet military threat began to disappear in its acute form after the collapse of the Soviet Union and the fall of its protégé in Kabul, despite the gradual improvement of ties between China and the Soviet Union in the last years of the Soviet Union. In the post–Soviet era, Russia and China have become major economic partners. Interesting enough, Russia has become the major supplier of advanced weapons to China in its process of military modernization. Through a verity of agreements signed since the mid-1990s, Russia has provided China with Kilo submarines and Sokhoi 27 and 30 fighter aircraft, for example.[27]

Chinese-Russian growing ties are friendly, but they are yet to become close allies, as both are seeking to establish themselves as global nuclear powers. The latter also applies to China's relations with India with two major differences: Their overall relations, although not hostile, are far from reliable and friendly, and their economic relations are still very insignificant. In such a situation, China does not wish to see Afghanistan leaning toward its active and potential enemies. The memory of a pro-Soviet Afghanistan is still fresh in the Chinese mind. In short, the Chinese should have every reason to be concerned about the concentration of military forces of regional or nonregional countries in Afghanistan, at least until the time when the Afghan military has grown strong enough to become a threat itself.

China has also been concerned about the possible negative impact of political uncertainty in Afghanistan on its stability. China shares a short border with its neighboring Afghanistan, which puts a geographical limit on the impact of positive or negative developments in that country. However, the Chinese have been concerned about the "export" of religious fundamentalism and political extremism from that country to their troubled Sinkiang Province, which neighbors Afghanistan.

For about three decades, Sinkiang Province has been the scene of ethnic conflict and anti-government activities.[28] The original inhabitants of Sinkiang Province are different Turkic ethnic groups. The Uyghurs account for the majority of the province's indigenous population, while the Kazakhs and the Kyrgyz form large communities. Dissatisfied with their treatment by the ethnic Chinese for a long time, the Uyghurs have expressed their dissatisfaction in a variety of ways, including efforts toward independence from China and the creation of an Uyghur state called Uyghuristan. Concerned about its impact on China's political stability and territorial integrity, the Chinese government has resorted to different means to eliminate the separatist threat. Thus, it has encouraged the migration of ethnic Chinese from other Chinese provinces to Sinkiang in a bid to change the latter's ethnic balance in favor of the Chinese. Nowadays, ethnic Chinese (about 8 million) outnumber the Uyghurs (about 7 million). As well, the Chinese government has resorted to the forcible assimilation of the Uyghurs into ethnic Chinese. These policies have created resentment among the Uyghurs who feel threatened culturally and ethnically, pushing them more toward expressing Uyghur nationalism in different forms.

Contrary to the intention of the Chinese government over the last two decades, its policies toward Uyghurs have worsened the situation in their province. Instead of removing the threat of instability and separatism, those policies have actually provoked the reverse. There has been a surge in anti-government activities among the Uyghurs that have taken both peaceful and violent forms. The disintegration of the Soviet Union, which led to the emergence of independent states of Kazakhstan and Kyrgyzstan along the Sinkiang border, has further encouraged such activities. Having large Uyghur communities, the rise of these "Turkic" states dominated by Turkic ethnic groups (the Kazakhs and the Kyrgyz, respectively) has increased the feasibility of independence as a political objective among the Uyghurs. The result has been the growth of their independence movement since 1991.

The Chinese government has implemented a zero-tolerance policy toward any forms of dissent in Sinkiang Province since the 1970s. Its harsh suppression of any type of political activity, regardless of its aim or form, has included the arrest and imprisonment of thousands of dissidents and activists as well as the execution of many others accused of armed struggle and/or advocating independence from China. Despite its systematic suppression of dissent, the Chinese government has failed to uproot opposition in Sinkiang Province. The indiscriminate suppression of all forms of unauthorized political activities, peaceful and violent alike, has increased the popularity and the legitimacy of the pro-independence movement among the alienated and dissatisfied Uyghurs, while securing international condemnations especially by human rights organizations such as Amnesty International.[29]

Thus, China has been afraid of any development in the proximity of Sinkiang Province with a potential worsening impact on the situation. The two-decade-long civil war in Afghanistan was a source of anxiety for the Chinese, especially because the war-torn country, in the absence of a fully functional Afghan government, became potentially suitable for a variety of destructive activities against China. The existence of a wide range of armed Mujahedin groups with extremist and/or fundamentalist orientations, which controlled different parts of Afghanistan as de facto independent rulers, created grounds for the free flow of arms and extremist views from that country into China.

The emergence of the Taliban and their rapid expansion to control almost the entire country was a blessing in disguise for the Chinese, although they subscribed to a very fundamentalist interpretation of Islam. China's friendly ties with Pakistan, the Taliban's mentor, ensured the cooperation of the group then in control of most parts of Afghanistan. This meant that the Taliban did not seek to destabilize China by allowing anti-Chinese subversive activities. Not only that, thanks to the Pakistanis, in December 1998, the Taliban allowed the Chinese to unearth an unexploded American cruise missile to improve their missile technology.[30] The missile was left intact since the American government launched a missile attack against an al-Qaeda camp in August 1998 following the bombing of two American embassies in Africa. In April 1999, the Chinese government sent a team to Afghanistan to bring the missile to China.[31] However, the Taliban failed to control the country fully and thus the destabilizing civil war continued. The continuation of civil war with an uncertain future was a source of concern for the Chinese. The Taliban's fall and the end of civil war addressed that concern only for a short while. As will be discussed in Chapter 3, the persistence of instability in Afghanistan has created grounds for the resumption of civil war in the future, which could be even more destructive and threatening.

Significance for Iran

Iran's ties with Afghanistan date back a few thousands years. Until about four hundred years ago, Afghanistan was part of Iran for which the two neighbors share a long period of common history. Additionally, thanks to their long common borders facilitating social contacts and also the presence of over 2 million Afghan refugees in Iran for over two decades, there are strong ethnic, linguistic, cultural, and religious ties between the two nations despite the separation of Afghanistan from Iran. As a result, instability, chaos, and criminal activities in Afghanistan could spill easily over into Iran. Unsurprisingly, the Iranians have watched their Afghan neighbors and have been concerned about the pace of events in their country with the potential of inducing instability in Iran.

Nevertheless, the roots of Iran's current policy toward its eastern neighbor should be traced back to the 1978 military coup in Afghanistan and its following Soviet invasion. During its last year in power, the Shah regime helped create the Iranian-based Afghan Mujahedin groups tasked with overthrowing the Soviet-backed regime put in power in 1978. Apart from the Iranian regime's anti-Soviet orientation because of Iran's pro-American stance, fear of a gradual encirclement by pro-Soviet neighbors and the expansion of Iranian underground Communist groups made the Shah regime react quickly to a sudden political development in its neighboring country. The 1979 Iranian revolution disrupted the Iranian society and changed the nature of the Iranian regime radically, but it did not affect Iran's commitment to the Afghan Mujahedin groups. On the contrary, the new Iranian government sharply increased its support to those groups of which many, excluding mainly Pashtun groups, set their headquarters in Iran. Pakistan emerged as the main base for the Pashtun Mujahedin, a "natural" phenomenon given the existence of a large Pashtun ethnic group in Pakistan's territory neighboring Afghanistan, the North-West Frontier Province (NWFP). With the exception of the ideological affinity with the Americans, the same reasons motivating the Shah regime to help create and support the Mujahedin groups remained the leading objectives behind Iran's continued support of them. The religious nature of the new Iranian government provided an additional incentive for its support of those fighting the Afghan Communist regime under the banner of an anti-Communist Islamic movement.

The Soviet invasion of Afghanistan in December 1979 and its subsequent occupation of the entire country increased Iran's stake in engaging in that country. Having a long border in the north with the Soviet Union (over 2,000 kilometers), Iran could not afford to be indifferent to the stationing of the Soviet troops in its neighboring country with which it shared about 1,000 kilometers of border. The growing influence of the Soviets in certain countries in Iran's vicinity left no doubt in the Iranians' mind about the necessity of removing the Soviet threat from Afghanistan. This Soviet influence was increasing among Pakistan's Baluchi tribes living along the Pakistani-Iranian border in the Province of Baluchistan, while their presence was expanding in another neighboring country, Iraq. Besides political factors, the Soviet Union's role as the largest arms supplier of Iraq then at war with Iran made the growing Soviet presence in Iran's vicinity especially alarming. No wonder if Iran emerged as one of the two major regional supporters of the Mujahedin groups along with Pakistan. It also became the country of refuge for over 2 million Afghans fleeing war and the economic hardship of living in their war-torn, devastated country.

The 1989 withdrawal of the Soviet troops paved the way for the eventual fall of the pro-Soviet regime of Afghanistan. In June 1992, the Mujahedin forces captured Kabul and ended the government of President Najibullah. The creation of a coalition government consisting of all the major Mujahedin groups did not last very long due to ethnic rivalry and its manipulation by foreign powers. As the main backer of the Pashtuns and its main Mujahedin group (Hizb-i Islami) led by Golbaddin Hekmatiar, Pakistan's efforts to control the entire country through a Pashtun-dominated Afghan government pitted it against Iran. For certain reasons, Iran favored a coalition government in which all ethnic groups were represented, including its Tajik, Hazara, and Uzbek protégés. They included its fear of Pakistan's domination over its neighboring country and of a new round of civil war this time between and among the Mujahedin groups, both pro-government and those dissatisfied with the governments' ethnic makeup. Aside from the civil war's destabilizing impact on Iran, the Iranian government was fearful of a predictable new massive inflow of Afghans into its country, with not only economic implications but also social and security ones.

For the next two years, the two Afghan rival camps supported by Iran and Pakistan engaged in a devastating war in their bid to achieve their objective: creating an Afghan regime dominated by one specific group and its allies through the elimination of other contenders or by forcing them to accept its authority. Many short-term coalitions formed between and among all Mujahedin groups, which lacked internal cohesion and clear ideological and political orientations. Coalition members switched loyalty to enemies frequently, an additional factor that deepened ethnic and political hatred and rivalry. As mentioned earlier, the Afghans' frustration with the chaotic situation caused by the civil war and its main protagonists provided grounds for the formation of the Taliban.

The emergence of the Taliban with its extremist and reactionary political views and its promotion of the harshest form of religious fundamentalism was a rising threat not only to all the Afghan rival groups now demonized by the Taliban, but also to Iran. Openly anti-Iranian, the group managed to capture the Pashtun regions, dismantle the local governments of the Mujahedin groups and warlords, and advance to the north very easily within two years after its formation in 1994. That type of performance was a clear outcome of its strong financial and military capabilities vis-à-vis other Afghan groups because of the generous support of Saudi Arabia, the UAE, Pakistan, and the United States to a differing extent and for a different period of time. In its northward advancement, it captured Kabul in 1996 after two years of on-and-off war, which pushed hundreds of thousands of Afghans into Iran, the home for about 2 million Afghan refugees. In such a situation, two factors created particular anxiety in Tehran. One was the growing burden of Afghan refugees on Iran, given there was no sign of an end to their inflow as long as the civil war continued. It was a horrifying situation for a country with massive economic problems caused by the 1979 revolution, its devastating eight-year war with Iraq in the 1980s, various economic sanctions, and the mismanagement of its economy. Another factor was the advancement of the Taliban in all directions, which led to their capture of Afghan provinces along the Iranian border formerly controlled by the pro-Iranian Tajik groups led by Ismail Khan.

The Taliban's advancement between 1996 and 1999 pitted Iran against not only the Taliban, but also its supporters as reflected in their uneasy, if not hostile in cases, bilateral relations. During that time, the Taliban imposed a devastating bloody war on the rest of Afghanistan controlled by the anti-Taliban Tajiki, Uzbek, Hazara, and Pashtun forces. In particular, the Taliban massive northern campaign in 1998 was a devastating blow to Iran and a clear success for its rival states backing the Taliban. The campaign pushed the anti-Taliban forces out of most of their areas and confined them to a territory in the north constituting about 10 percent of the Afghan land. The anti-Iranian Taliban were bad news for Iran from the first day of their emergence, but it became worse in 1998 when, through phenomenal atrocities, they emerged as the ruler of most parts of Afghanistan. Their massacre of two predominately Shiite cities of Taligan and Bamian and their capture of Mazar-i-Sharif, the stronghold of the Uzbek groups and a major base for other anti-Taliban forces, were both a political defeat and a security threat to Iran. As well, they were a source of embarrassment for Iran's Shiite government, which seemed unable to help its religious kin and political protégés. The Taliban's murder of seven Iranian diplomats and a few other Iranians in Mazar-i-Sharif led to an Iranian show of force along its border with Afghanistan in 1998.[32]

Russia and India also shared Iran's concern about the Taliban's rapid expansion and their bid to capture the rest of Afghanistan's territory along its border with Central Asia. The three regional powers could not accept Pakistan's total control of Afghanistan both for political and economic reasons and security considerations. Beside its objective of turning itself into a strong regional power, Pakistan was clearly seeking to secure its free access to Central Asia through its Afghan protégé, a region of importance to the three regional powers. One of its major objectives was to turn itself into the major route for international trade and, particularly, for export of oil and gas from Central Asia. If realized, that route would enable the Central Asians to bypass both Iran and Russia, a plan also supported by the American government concerned about the two countries and their influence in Central Asia for different reasons. Moreover, the advancement of the fundamentalist Taliban with their desire to export their subversive political and religious ideology was a threat to the stability of the Central Asian countries and a potential one to Russia fearful of the radicalization of its dissatisfied Muslim ethnic groups. The common political, economic, and security concerns pushed Iran, India, and Russia closer to each other. The three states became the main force behind the Northern Alliance through which they sought to reverse the political tide in Afghanistan, a commitment lasting to this day.

Beside political and economic considerations, an unstable Afghanistan is a threat to Iran for other reasons. They include Afghanistan-based international drug-trafficking and related illegal activities, which have been a major source of concern for Iran especially since the early 1980s. The continuation and phenomenal expansion of illegal drug activity was an additional threat for the Iranians during the Taliban regime and a major contributing factor to their hostility toward it. Drug-traffickers' efforts to cross the Iranian border and their constant fighting with Iranian border troops and law enforcement forces resulted in significant losses in human lives (3,350 persons by 1998) beside its heavy financial cost. According to the Iranian authorities, the annual cost of anti-narcotic operations was about $400 million in the 1990s.[33] Afghanistan-based drug-trafficking also became a serious contributing factor to instability along the Iranian-Afghan border. With a government estimation of 2 million drug addicts, the rapid expansion of drug addiction in Iran created not only health, but also alarming social problems for the Iranians.[34] To this picture, one should add the expansion of violent crimes associated with drug-trafficking, such as small arms trafficking, armed robbery and banditry, to appreciate the depth of security threat of Afghanistan-based drug-trafficking for Iran.

International drug-trafficking aside, instability in Afghanistan under the Taliban regime created social and economic problems for Iran, because it caused a massive migration of Afghans to Iran, which already had a large Afghan refugee population. Over two decades of civil war in Afghanistan has created a large Afghan refugee population, the majority of whom live in Iran and Pakistan. Iran has been the host to over 2 million Afghans for this period; this has been a huge financial burden on its government. Iran's two decades of economic problems caused by the 1979 revolution, the eight-year war with Iraq, various economic sanctions, and the mismanagement of economy have limited its economic means, while requiring a huge amount of investment in its economy to meet its own population's needs. Given this situation, the cost of taking care of a large refugee population has been a drain on Iran's limited resources. The atrocities committed by the Taliban against the Afghan civilians, and particularly against the non-Pashtun civilians who escaped en masse from areas falling into Taliban control, removed the possibility of the voluntary repatriation of the Afghans beyond token efforts. Creating new refugees and perpetuating the residence of millions of Afghans in Iran, the Taliban regime became yet another source of social and economic problems for the Iranian government.

Besides these reasons, Iran has had two major concerns about Afghanistan. One has been its fear that Afghanistan will turn into an enemy state and/or become a base for Iran's enemies. This has arisen from the Iranians' fear of their total encirclement by hostile neighbors. Especially, the latter was the case during the 1980s when all their neighbors were on hostile terms with them when Iran was at war with Iraq. The war ended in 1988, but Iraq remained an enemy despite the ceasefire and the existence of a degree of diplomatic relations. An unreliable and fragile no-war, no-peace situation between the two countries has continued to this date despite Saddam Hussein's fall. The collapse of the Soviet Union changed the situation along Iran's northern border to some extent. With the exception of

Russia, suspicions about the revolutionary Iranian government initially made the newly independent states reluctant to open up to Iran although they did not create an immediate security threat to Iran.[35] Over time, Iran has established peaceful and friendly ties with all its new neighbors excluding Azerbaijan whose relations with Iran has gone through problematic, unfriendly, and hostile periods.[36]

A western neighbor of Iran along with Iraq, in the early 1990s Turkey began to normalize its ties with Iran. Those relations were damaged by the 1979 revolution and worsened during the 1980s when Turkey practically sided with Iraq. They began to improve in the 1990s. In addition to economic contracts, the two sides concluded agreements on security in 1992 and 1993[37] and on border security and crackdowns on each state's opposition groups based in the other country in 1994.[38] Although those relations have since been stable and peaceful, the two countries are still far from reliable and predictable friends. Given Iran's troubled relations with the United States, the existence of American military bases in Turkey has been a source of worry for the Iranians. The conflicting interests of the two neighbors in the Caucasus and Central Asia have also contributed to their current state of relations.

To a varying extent, Iran's relations with its southern neighbors, that is, Arab Persian Gulf countries (Saudi Arabia, Kuwait, Qatar, Bahrain, Oman, and the UAE), were unfriendly or hostile in the 1980s. Iran's real or perceived support of their anti-regime forces and their support of Iraq then at war with Iran created grounds for mistrust, suspicion, and hostility on both sides. The bilateral ties began to improve only after the Iraqi invasion of Kuwait and the subsequent 1991 Persian Gulf war. Iran's siding with the Kuwaitis and the Saudis and its refusal to assist Iraq helped put their ties with the Iranians on a friendly path; other Arab Persian Gulf states gradually followed suit. Nevertheless, Iran's ties with all its southern neighbors became friendly and stable only after the 1997 election of Mohammad Khatami as president. His pursuit of a foreign policy aimed at tension reduction and improving ties with foreign countries paved the way for full normalization of Iranian relations with its southern neighbors as well as many other countries near and far.[39] However, the existence of American military bases in Saudi Arabia, Kuwait, Oman, and Bahrain was and still is a major potential threat for Iran, making its ties with those nations somewhat problematic. The stationing of the American troops in Iraq and Qatar has increased that threat since early in 2003.

Iran's relations with Pakistan, its eastern neighbor, were also unreliable in the 1980s, although not overtly hostile. Under various international economic sanctions for different reasons, the two countries had extensive economic relations warranted by their ability to satisfy certain mutual needs. This situation continued in the 1990s despite their accusing each other of supporting armed and extremist opposition groups and of inducing sectarian violence.

Moreover, the two countries continued their diplomatic relations as well as economic and military ties despite their major conflicts over Afghanistan as the backers of opposing Mujahedin groups. Yet, their conflict worsened as Pakistan emerged as the mentor of the Taliban, a declared enemy of Iran. Thus, until the Taliban's fall, their proxy war in Afghanistan was the major source of conflict between the two neighbors, although they pursued normal relations, including economic ties, throughout that period. To a limited degree, Iranian-Pakistani relations have also been damaged because of their rivalry to establish themselves as the main transit route for the energy resources of the landlocked Central Asia. In short, having an overtly hostile neighbor (Iraq) and many unreliable and/or potentially hostile states around it, Iran could not accept a hostile Afghanistan along its eastern border.

Another major concern of Iran was Afghanistan's potential to "export" its instability to Central Asia, a region of great interest to the Iranians.[40] Afghanistan is an ethnic mirror of Central Asia. This social factor, on the one hand, and Afghanistan's long border with three Central Asian states, on the other, make the spillover of instability from Afghanistan to Central Asia a feasible scenario. This very realistic possibility is due to the existence of a suitable situation for the rise of mass dissent in Central Asia. Factors contributing to such a situation include numerous transitional problems, extensive human rights abuses, rampant corruption, growing poverty, high unemployment, and authoritarianism.[41] Consequently, Iran's concern about instability in Afghanistan was worsened significantly by the Taliban. This sensitivity has remained in place since the collapse of the Taliban regime.

Significance for Pakistan

Since its independence in 1947, Pakistan has had strong interests in Afghanistan for at least two major reasons: its potential impact on the stability and security of Pakistan, and also for a crucial role it could play to help Pakistan achieve certain regional and international objectives. Afghanistan could directly affect the stability of its neighboring Pakistan because of its ethnic ties to that country. Pakistan has a large Pashtun ethnic group living in its province neighboring Afghanistan, the NWFP. There is a direct ethnic tie between these Pashtuns and their kin in Afghanistan whose main concentration is in the south and southeast along the Afghan-Pakistani border. This natural ethnic link was a major factor in Pakistan's backing of Pashtun Mujahedin groups in Afghanistan during the 1980s and the 1990s and also for its creation and support of the Pashtun-dominated Taliban.

Stability in Afghanistan is of crucial importance for Pakistan because of its direct impact on Pakistan's stability. The direct ethnic ties between the two countries and the geographical realities make the expansion of instability from Afghanistan into Pakistan a very feasible scenario. As recognized by the Pakistani constitution, the autonomous status of the Pashtun-dominated tribal area of the NWFP keeps those areas along the border with Afghanistan practically out of the Pakistani government's control. This reality makes that government worry about the rise of instability in Afghanistan, which could easily destabilize the northern part of its country run by the tribal leaders with questionable loyalty to their central government. For this matter, the Pakistani government cannot remain indifferent to instability in Afghanistan.

Afghanistan is also important for Pakistan as it could help the Pakistanis achieve certain objectives. One major area is its national security. A pro-Pakistani Afghanistan would alleviate Pakistan's security concern. It is a "natural" concern for a country neighboring India, a huge hostile nuclear state to its east with which it has fought three major wars since their independence in 1947. To the west, it has Iran as a neighbor. Being a good friend of India, that neighbor is a large and rich regional power and a rival of Pakistan. Iranian-Pakistani relations have not experienced a long period of hostility, but they have been on occasions unfriendly and unreliable. This is a consequence of their conflicting national interests in the region, their antagonistic interests in Afghanistan, and their very different foreign policies. Having Afghanistan under its control, Pakistan could be certain about security along its long north and northeastern borders with Afghanistan. In such a case, the Pakistani government could prevent its country's encirclement from three sides by enemies or potential enemies. That type of security relief would help the Pakistanis use their limited resources to strengthen their military forces facing those of India, the active "traditional" enemy of Pakistan. Despite its limited advanced weapons, India's very large conventional military force (1 million strong) mostly concentrated along its border with Pakistan, poses a very serious threat to Pakistan as experienced in its lost wars with India in 1948, 1965, and 1971.

As well, Afghanistan is important for the Pakistanis for the role it could play in advancing their national interests in the regions in Pakistan's proximity. First, Afghanistan could help the Pakistanis strengthen themselves by offering them the opportunity to expand their influence in West Asia. By dominating Afghanistan through its Afghan protégé, Pakistan could expand its power and influence in that region. The result would be a stronger position for Pakistan in its rivalry with both Iran and India, which are also interested in the same region. Second, Pakistan's domination over Afghanistan would weaken two major regional powers befriended with India (i.e., Iran and Russia). Their weakness would indirectly weaken India's position in its own region, that is South Asia, and also in West Asia by denying the Indians the assistance of those regional powers sharing most of their strategic views and objectives. As Pakistan experienced firsthand during the Taliban era, a pro-Pakistani and anti-Iranian/anti-Russian Afghan regime could create a wide range of problems, including security threats for Iran. Among other problems, a pro-Pakistani Afghanistan would destabilize Iran's bordering area with Afghanistan and create a constant security threat for the Iranians. In fact, this was a major source of anxiety for Iran during the Taliban era. Facing such threat, security imperatives would force Iran to spend a huge amount of its economic resources on dealing with the threats initiating from Afghanistan, as it actually did when the Taliban were in power. The same type of threat would also lock a significant part of the Iranian military force along Iran's long border with Afghanistan. This would be a blessing in disguise for Pakistan as it cannot afford economically and militarily to face two hostile forces along its eastern and western borders.

Although Russia does not share borders with Afghanistan, a pro-Pakistani Afghan government could create security concerns for it as well. Instability caused by such a government for the Central Asian countries could also destabilize Russia, as the former share a long border with Russia. Given various social, economic, political, and geographical ties between these countries and Russia, instability in Central Asia could feasibly expand to Russia, a source of concern for the Russians for about a decade. Such a concern was a major objective for Russia to support the Northern Alliance along with Iran and India.

Finally, for its geographical position, Afghanistan also offers the Pakistanis the opportunity to address some of their economic problems and to uplift their international status. Sandwiched between Central Asia and Pakistan, that country could enable the Pakistanis to secure access to the Central Asian countries with which they have no common border. Provided there is a pro-Pakistani government in Kabul, a friendly and docile Afghanistan can turn Pakistan into a route for the international trade of the landlocked Central Asian countries. Any amount of Central Asian trade conducted via the Pakistani route would be a welcoming economic activity for the Pakistanis, because it would provide income in transit fees and generate long-term employment. Nevertheless, Pakistan has hoped to establish its route for the lucrative and prestigious export of Caspian oil and natural gas.[42] In that capacity, it could offer a transit route for the oil and natural gas exports of Kazakhstan and Turkmenistan, the two major energy-rich Central Asian countries aspiring to export large amounts of fossil energy in the future. As well, it could offer its route to Uzbekistan, a Central Asian country with much smaller oil and gas resources, but still with an export capability currently used to a limited extent. Pakistan's functioning as an energy route would generate for the Pakistanis a larger amount of annual revenues and a larger number of well-paid employment opportunities on a long-term basis than they could possibly hope by availing their route for the Central Asians' nonenergy trade. These are two necessities for the cash-starved Pakistan with an inadequate number of jobs for the growing number of its job applicants.

Moreover, Pakistan's role as a main, if not the main, oil and gas export route would elevate its international status with direct positive impacts not only on its economy, but also on its security. Without a doubt, those states involved in the development and export of the Caspian fossil energy resources as well as the importing countries would have a strong stake in the stability of Pakistan and of its region, if they relied on that country for their imported energy requirements. Given the American dominant position in the development of the Central Asian energy industry and the American interest in an export route to bypass Iran and Russia, a fully-functional Pakistani route would create stakes for the United States in the stability and the security of Pakistan. In part, it would require Pakistan's economic growth to deal with a main source of social instability, that is, its poor economic situation resulting in rampant poverty. Functioning in that capacity, Pakistan would be in a much stronger position vis-à-vis its enemies and rivals, especially India, the single largest source of threat for the Pakistanis. In particular, such a situation might prevent the worst case scenario for Pakistan (i.e., the United States taking sides with India in the Indian-Pakistani conflict over disputed Kashmir). This has been a major fear of the Pakistanis who have every reason to believe that, in the end, the Americans might choose India, and not Pakistan, as their regional ally. While India may have a different idea about its strategic alliances, this is a realistic possibility given India's certain characteristics that make it a more attractive ally for the Americans. They include its vast area, its large and growing population, its emerging advancement in high tech and pharmaceuticals, and its long joint borders with the rising nuclear power, China. To this list, one should add India's more impressive nuclear capability and its potential for growth.[43] In conclusion, for various reasons, Afghanistan could help Pakistan address some of its national, regional, and international objectives. For that matter, Pakistan has had vested interests in Afghanistan at least over the last two decades.

Significance for India

India lacks a common border with Afghanistan, but it also has stakes in that country. However, they are mainly unrelated to the country itself, as Afghanistan is not significant for the Indians for its own merits. This is a result of its devastating situation after over two decades of war, which makes it unattractive for India in search of markets. Also, this is an outcome of its lack of technological advancement and strong financial capability, two major needs of India in the foreseeable future. Against this background, the Indians have three major reasons for their interest in Afghanistan. They all reflect their objective of denying their archenemies, the Pakistanis, the opportunity to enhance their power and to seek their regional objectives.

First, India has sought to deny Pakistan domination over Afghanistan. As mentioned earlier, for various reasons, Afghanistan could help Pakistan address some of its needs and strengthen its power in the region, while uplifting its regional and international status. If successful in securing its objectives there, a stronger and more confident Pakistan will undoubtedly be a more dangerous enemy for India. It will also be more aggressive in pursuing its regional interests with a predictable outcome of weakening India's power and influence in South and West Asia. In this regard, a clear recent example was Pakistan's boasted morale and self-confidence reflected in its pursuit of a blatant aggressive policy in Afghanistan less than three months after its May 1998 nuclear tests. Aimed at expanding the Taliban's authority all over Afghanistan by eliminating their opponents supported by Iran, India, and Russia, the Pakistanis encouraged and supported the Taliban to conduct their massive northward campaign in Afghanistan in July 1998. During its course, they committed extensive atrocities against the civilian population, including the massacre of the residents of Bamian, Taligan, and Mazar-i-Sharif. Like many other anti-Taliban states, India and Iran accused the Pakistani government of direct involvement in the operation. For example, Dr. Rohani, Secretary of the Supreme National Security Council of Iran, referred to "undeniable" evidence indicating that government's leading role in the operation.[44]

To avoid such a scenario, India has sought to deny Pakistan the opportunity to strengthen itself through its domination of Afghanistan. As a result, along with Iran and Russia, but to a much lesser extent, India assisted the anti-Taliban Northern Alliance during its fight against the Taliban regime. Besides military aid, such assistance included its establishing a hospital in Farkhor in Tajikistan, which is close to the Tajik-Afghan border. The Alliance troops used the hospital for their medical needs.[45]

Second, India has been concerned especially about Pakistan's bid to expand its influence in Central Asia. This is partly due to its interest in keeping Pakistan out of a region where it also seeks political influence and economic gains. It is also partly because of its fear of a stronger Pakistan. Provided Afghanistan's cooperation, Central Asia could boost Pakistan's economy, leaving the Pakistanis in a much better financial situation. Among other programs, it would enable them to embark on ambitious military programs to upgrade and to expand their conventional forces, which are far inferior to those of India. As well, more prosperous Pakistanis would have financial means to pursue certain interrelated objectives, namely enlarging their nuclear arsenal, which is smaller than that of India, and revitalizing their missile program to develop medium- and long-range missiles. Their lack is a great handicap for the Pakistani nuclear force.[46]

Finally, India has been concerned about the negative impact on Iran and Russia of the growing influence of Pakistan in Afghanistan. The latter have been its two major regional friends sharing many of its regional and international concerns. Security threats arising from Afghanistan have been a major source of preoccupation for the two countries over the last two decades. Those threats have taken different forms, including the training and operation of extremist groups hostile to the two countries in Afghanistan and the trafficking of narcotics and small arms from Afghanistan to and through their countries with health and security hazards for them. Such threats, which have continued to this date despite the Taliban's fall, have an obvious weakening impact on the two countries. Instability in Iran and Russia and their economic and political weaknesses will not only deny India two regional friends, but will dash its hope for a substantial amount of annual revenue and political influence, which it hopes to gain through the trilateral North-South Corridor Agreement (NSCA).[47] If fully implemented, this agreement has the potential to boost India's economy and change its international status.

Iran, India, and Russia agreed in late 2000 to begin a trial period, followed by their May 2002 signing of an official agreement. The NSCA envisages the creation of mainly a land link between Europe and Asia as an alternative to the widely used route via the Mediterranean Sea and the Suez Canal. Currently, the main intercontinental transit route is a land/sea one via the Suez Canal. Through a combination of land means of transportation (trains and trucks), that route connects Europe's markets to the European ports whereby cargoes are carried to Asian destinations by sea vessels via the Suez Canal. Along with its high cost and long length, the route passes through the troubled Middle East where instability may even lead to the canal's complete closure for an unpredictable period of time, a realistic consequence of a regional war.

The NSCA provides for a transport corridor connecting the Indian Ocean with the Baltic Sea through India's port of Mumbai (formerly Bombay) and Russia's port of St. Petersburg via Iran. Accordingly, from Mumbai, Indian and other Asian products carried to India by sea or land are shipped to Iran's Persian Gulf port of Bandar Abbas. From there, they are transported by trucks and/or train connecting Bandar Abbas with the Caspian Sea ports of Bandar Anzali and Bandar Amirabad via Tehran. At those ports, cargoes are carried across the Caspian Sea to Russia's port of Astrakhan linked via road and rail to the Baltic Sea port of St. Petersburg through Volgagrad and Moscow. From St. Petersburg, cargoes are shipped to their final European destinations and European products carried to that port are transported to India via Iran. India is currently connecting its rail network to those of Myanmar and Thailand. Once that rail link is operational, the transit corridor will provide the shortest and cheapest trade link between Asia and Europe. Currently, the route reduces the intercontinental transit time from fifteen to twenty days via the Suez Canal to ten to twelve days as it decreases the trade route's length between Europe to Asia from 16,129 kilometers to 6,245 kilometers. For this reason, it significantly brings down the cost of cargo transportation between the two continents.

The underlying idea behind the NSCA is to offer a safe, reliable, and inexpensive route to all those involved in the large Asian-European trade. Evidence indicates that this trade will grow on a steady basis, as Asia will be the largest global market of the twenty-first century. The continent has all the ingredients for growth, including a large and growing population, vast mineral and fossil energy resources, an increasing technological capability, and a strong desire for economic development. They all have contributed to the formation of a large, expanding, and undersatisfied market.

There is no doubt that the Asian market will be the engine of growth for the global economy in the twenty-first century. This is a logical result of certain trends. They are the shrinkage of the European market because of its decreasing and ageing population, the disappearance of the African market (excluding its northern part and South Africa) due to endless wars and natural disasters, and the stagnation or shrinkage of the South American economy. Given this situation, the large and growing European-Asian trade will require reliable and, preferably, inexpensive transport routes, a reality on which the NSCA seeks to capitalize. Provided Iran, India, and Russia expand and upgrade their transportation infrastructure and reach agreements with major European and Asian trading nations, the NSCA can generate for them hundreds of millions of dollars in annual incomes. Their annual revenue in transit fees could increase to billions of dollars in the long run as a result of the full utilization of their cargo transit infrastructure and the anticipated growth of the major Asian economies. The agreement could also create hundreds of thousands of jobs for Iran, India, and Russia with a large army of the unemployed. For the time being, a few countries, mainly CIS ones, use this link for a relatively low volume of cargo.

Without a doubt, the NSCA has the potential to facilitate and expand international trade and bring substantial economic and political benefits for Iran, India, and Russia. If fully implemented and if the three countries fully develop their transportation infrastructure, the agreement will be a major contribution to their economic growth, which has been hampered as a result of factors such as their limited financial resources. In short, the NSCA has the potential to turn Iran, India, and Russia into the hub of the Asian-European cargo transportation route, while uplifting their international status and political influence.

Significance for Russia

Russia's interest in Afghanistan can be traced back to the Soviet era. At that time, four main factors made the Soviet leaders interested in their neighboring country. First, there was a security concern. The Soviet leaders wanted to relieve the security pressure on their country caused by their having hostile (China) or unreliable noncommunist and pro-American countries

(Iran and Turkey) along their long southern borders. For that matter, having a friendly and pro-Soviet Afghanistan would have helped them decrease the security threat along their southern border. As well, it would have prevented the Soviet Union's complete encirclement by hostile or potentially hostile countries. Second, there was a long-term concern about the possible destabilizing impact on their Central Asian republics of Afghanistan, a country with similar ethnic makeup to those republics. This ethnic link created grounds for a free flow of destabilizing political ideas and ideologies. Hence, it became necessary to secure the friendly attitude of Afghanistan toward its northern neighbor as well as to ensure its security and stability. Third, as a by-product of their domination in that country, the Soviet leaders were interested in Afghanistan's natural gas resources. Because of its limited gas reserves, Afghanistan was not, and still is not, a major gas exporter. However, its resources were significant enough to address some of the fuel needs of the Soviet Central Asian republics for awhile. Those republics had significant, but mostly undeveloped, gas reserves. With these ideas and concerns in mind, the Soviet leaders helped the pro-Soviet Afghans stage a coup in 1978. The inability of their regime to control its country and consolidate its own power forced the Soviets to send their troops to Afghanistan, as mentioned earlier. The new situation gave birth to a fourth factor creating an interest for the Soviets in Afghanistan: ensuring the survival of their protégé.

The fall of the Soviet Union and the collapse of the pro-Soviet regime in Afghanistan changed the situation to a limited extent. For a short while, the prevailing view in the Russian elite about Russian foreign policy made the Russians uninterested in Asian countries, including Afghanistan. That view advocated a pro-Western approach in Russia's foreign policy at the expense of cutting or limiting ties with other countries, including even former Soviet republics in Asia.[48] In particular, the prevailing anti-Asian mood in the Russian government, which described the Asian Soviet republics as a drain on the Russian economy, left no room for any interest in those republics, let alone Afghanistan where the Soviets experienced a nine-year bloody war. As the Russians became disillusioned about receiving significant help from the West, Russia's economic realities requiring trade with the CIS countries bankrupted this view. The Russian government became interested again in the Central Asian republics and their stability. Moreover, Russia's fear about security threats initiated in the countries along its southern borders, including western-sponsored ones, and the growing instability in the Caucasus and Central Asia reflected in civil wars in those regions, interested the Russians in their former Asian republics. For these reasons, stability in Afghanistan became important for Russia for its impact on its neighboring Central Asia and, particularly, for its potential of exporting instability to the Central Asian republics. The latter now became important to Russia for economic, political, and military/security reasons. Furthermore, the Russian government was also concerned about the negative impact of instability in Central Asia and Afghanistan on its own country. Unstable Central Asia and Afghanistan could "export" instability to Russia, a country with a large number of ethnic minorities with a variety of economic, political, social, and historical reasons for grievances with Moscow. Hence, the continuation of civil war in Afghanistan with its destabilizing impact on Central Asia and Russia became a major source of concern for Russia, and it worsened when the Taliban regime came to power.

In the 1990s, the security concern became the main reason for Russia's interest in Afghanistan. During that period, the Russians sought to ensure peace and stability in their own country. They were the major requirements for their predictably long process of addressing their numerous economic, social, and political problems. As discussed earlier, Russia joined Iran as the main supporters of the Northern Alliance to prevent the northward expansion of the Taliban's destructive political views and to stabilize Afghanistan eventually through a more reliable and predictable Afghan government with a friendly attitude toward Russia.

In the post–Taliban era, at least two Russian interests in Afghanistan have remained well in place. Of these, one is Russia's stake in ensuring stability in Afghanistan to prevent the spillover of instability from that country to Central Asia and possibly further to the north to Russia. As a by-product of a prolonged period of instability and lawlessness in Afghanistan, Afghanistan-based international drug-trafficking has also become a major source of concern for Russia, both for its expanding health hazards and also for its contribution to criminal activities in Russia. According to a 2001 estimate, the existence of between 3 and 4 million drug addicts demonstrates the depth of the problem for the Russian government.[49]

The other interest is Russia's need to have a friendly Afghanistan to avoid its encirclement by hostile states. Having lost mostly to the American camp just about all its Soviet era's friends and allies, fear of a gradual process of encirclement by enemy or unreliable states close to its borders has made the Russian government concerned about the direction of political development in Afghanistan. Hence, Russia wants to ensure that Afghanistan will not turn into a base for anti-Russian states. This has become even more important now than it was in the Soviet era. Nowadays, Russia's numerous domestic problems make it highly vulnerable to foreign threats. In this regard, preventing the expansion of American political and military presence in Afghanistan and especially preventing its long-term stay there have become of special importance to the Russians. As most of their former republics both in Asia and Europe have become very close to the Western countries, in particular the United States, the Russians cannot afford any further expansion of American, political, economic, and military presence in their close proximity. In particular, in the post–Taliban era, the rapid expansion of American influence, including its military presence, along the southern Russian borders in the Central Asian and Caucasian countries has created a lot of justifiable anxiety in Russia. A pro-American Afghanistan hosting American military forces will only worsen the security threat to Russia.

Significance for the United States

The U.S. interests in Afghanistan had its roots in the Cold War rivalry between that country and the Soviet Union. The Americans became interested in Afghanistan as it suddenly slipped into the Soviet camp in 1978. As part of its efforts to stop the expansion of the Soviet bloc, the American government helped the Afghan Mujahedin groups along with Iran and Pakistan, the two regional countries hosting, training, and arming those groups. As discussed earlier, the American government remained interested in Afghanistan and continued backing the Mujahedin groups as long as fighting in Afghanistan helped its strategic objective of weakening its arch rival, the Soviet Union. Therefore, as a clear sign of a weakened Soviet Union, the withdrawal of the Soviet troops from that country in 1989 began to decrease the American interest in the country itself. The collapse of the Soviet Union, which deprived the Kabul regime of its only backer, practically terminated the American interest in Afghanistan, as it became quite clear that the fall of that regime was just a matter of time. In June 1992, the Mujahedin's capture of Kabul removed the pro-Soviet regime from the political scene and practically ended the strategic interest of the American government in Afghanistan.

Afghanistan regained its importance for the United States a few years later. The growing interest of the Americans in the fossil energy resources of the Caspian Sea region brought about the troublesome issue of finding reliable export routes for their long-term export to international markets. In their bid to find an alternative route to those of Iran and Russia, the Americans became interested in the Pakistani route passing through Afghanistan. Having access to open seas via its ports on the Arabian Sea, Pakistan could offer a desired route, but one of its major handicaps was unstable Afghanistan. As discussed before, that reality made the construction and long-term operation of any oil or gas pipeline passing through Afghanistan simply out of the question. The continuation of the Afghan civil war whose end was anybody's guess subjected the selection of the Pakistani route to the war's end and the formation of a fully-functional central government. The emergence of the Taliban created grounds for the achievement of the objective, as its full control of Afghanistan could make the use of the Pakistani route feasible. This possibility made the Americans interested in Afghanistan and also in the Taliban regime as a means toward that end. An agreement for the construction of a gas pipeline connecting Turkmenistan's gas fields to Pakistan via Afghanistan for meeting Pakistan's need for gas and for exporting Turkmen gas to other countries was signed in 1993 among Turkmenistan, Afghanistan, and Pakistan.[50] Unocal, an American oil company, headed a consortium of oil companies interested in the project.[51] Once the Taliban emerged on the political scene as a rising star, the company sought and received their cooperation. However, the failure of the Taliban to control the entire country and to end the civil war made the implementation of the pipeline project impossible. As a result, Unocal gave up the project in 1998 and closed down its operation in Central Asia in 1999.[52] Apart from the Taliban's clear inability to control the entire country, cooperation with the Taliban became impossible for Unocal as the American government banned any contact with the group in the aftermath of the bombing of two American embassies in Africa in 1998. The American government blamed Osama bin Laden and his organization (al-Qaeda) for masterminding the bombings and accused the Taliban of providing a safe haven for them. The subsequent American missile attack against a camp where bin Laden was thought to stay ended the ties between the American government and the Taliban in 1998.

In the post–Taliban era, the American interests in Afghanistan fall into two categories of short- and long-term interests. The short-term interests include those justified by certain immediate objectives. An obvious objective is the elimination of the terrorist groups based in that country, namely the remnants of al-Qaeda and the Taliban. Initially, the operation was to be over in less than a year. However, there is no sign of its end about two years after its beginning in October 2001. As expected by some military and political observers, the uprooting of the Afghan-based terrorist organizations would not be feasible in a short period of time given the loose nature of their organization and their fighting pattern (i.e., small-scale hit-and-run type of operation). Among other factors, their taking advantage of the receptive mood in the tribal-controlled parts of Pakistan's NWFP where they can seek refuge once they are under pressure in Afghanistan has further complicated the situation. Consequently, the 2002 American military announcement of a longer-than-expected stay of the American forces in Afghanistan did not surprise anyone. In his August 2002 meeting with Uzbek President Islam Karimov in Tashkent, the commander of the American forces in Afghanistan, Central Asia, and the Persian Gulf, General Tommy L. Franks, stated that the American military presence in Central Asia and Afghanistan would increase.[53] He also added that the American forces would stay longer than expected in Afghanistan.[54]

Beside the mentioned security objective, another short-term American objective is to ensure the stability of Afghanistan. Unless the country is fully stable, even the complete elimination of the existing terrorist groups will not mean the end of Afghanistan-based terrorism. In the absence of a fully-functional strong central government, civil war will likely be resumed in one form or another. The predictable chaos and lawlessness will create a suitable ground for the reemergence of the Taliban or like-minded groups offering sanctuary to the new or old international terrorist organizations to establish themselves in that country.

The American long-term interests in Afghanistan include certain interests justified by strategic objectives. These interests are geared to the country's geographical location. Given its position as a neighbor of Iran, China, and Pakistan, and its proximity to Russia and India, Afghanistan offers the United States the opportunity to pursue some of its strategic objectives. Added to the American forces now stationed in Central Asia (Kyrgyzstan and Uzbekistan) and in the Caucasus (Georgia), the American troops in Afghanistan can help their government seek to keep Iran and China in check. Being two regional powers, the American government is concerned about their regional and international objectives, which may conflict with those of its own. China is a nuclear power, but its nuclear arsenal is very insignificant compared to that of the United States both in terms of destructive capability and the means of delivery. However, as its economy expands and its technological capability improves, China becomes more assertive in expressing its views and pursuing its objectives requiring stronger conventional and nuclear capabilities. This will not be a serious threat to the United States in the foreseeable future. Yet, China's potential capability to emerge as a superpower in the long run has been a source of preoccupation for that country.

Iran is not a current military threat to the United States. Nor is it going to be one in the near future given its lack of a nuclear capability, a long-range missile system, and an extensive military satellite capability. Nevertheless, the American government is concerned about its long-term objectives. This is apart from their current grievances about its real or perceived threatening behavior summarized in what the Americans describe as its support of terrorism (mainly backing of Palestinian and Lebanese extremist groups), its opposition to the Israeli-Palestinian peace plan, and its alleged efforts to acquire nuclear weapons. As a rising regional power, the Americans are concerned about Iran's future objectives and its potential ability to pose a threat to their interests, if the current state of hostile relations between the two countries continues. As material preconditions to make that scenario feasible, Iran's certain characteristics have created grounds for a future phenomenal economic growth and a military expansion program. They include its large industrial basis, its abundance of mineral resources and fossil energy, its large educated population, and its significant financial capability.

The United States also seeks to contain India and Pakistan, although they are not a current threat to its security. The two countries will not be able to turn themselves into major powers capable of endangering American interests and/or posing a military threat to the United States, thanks to their certain deficiencies. The most visible of the latter are their enormous domestic political, economic, and social problems, their limited resources especially financial ones, their large and growing population, and their massive poverty. However, the Indian and Pakistani nuclear capabilities, despite their current insignificance compared to the American capability, have created grounds for concern about their potential long-term threat. Of course, that potential requires a prerequisite: the significant expansion of their nuclear arsenals and their acquisition of long-range missiles and/or extensive long-range aircraft fleets. Although the achievement of such capabilities in the short and medium term seems rather unlikely, the Americans should be concerned about the clear regional and especially international ambitions of the two states. Those ambitions motivated them to join the nuclear club in 1998 when they tested their nuclear weapons. Moreover, the historical grievances of the two states with the Western countries, including the United States, their political inclinations, and their "traditional" pattern of alliances have made a case for their possible turning against the Americans. Despite their current friendly ties with the United States and even Pakistan's alliance with that country in its war on Afghanistan-based terrorist groups, in the long run, India and Pakistan will likely align themselves in implicit or explicit forms with their traditional allies, Russia, and China. Hence, the American military deployment in Afghanistan, the southern CIS countries, and the Persian Gulf will also serve as a means to ensure the American government's ability to contain the two regional nuclear powers.

Containing Russia is yet another long-term objective of the Americans. The Cold War is long over and Russia and the United States are not on hostile terms. Yet, the post–Cold War era has made it clear that the Western countries, including the United States, have no incentive to help Russia address its numerous problems, particularly its phenomenal economic ones. Those problems facilitated the collapse of the Soviet Union and turned a superpower into a weak state. With a population of 146.2 million, Russia's low GDP of $401.4 billion in 1999 is almost equal to that of the Netherlands ($393.7 billion), a small country of 15.8 million.[55] The Western countries have every reason to prevent the re-rise of Russia as a fully-fledged superpower once it is too weak to pose a threat to them. This has been quite clear in the pattern of economic assistance provided by the Western countries for the former Soviet republics and bloc members. The amount of foreign financial assistance for Russia in the forms of loans, grants, and investments has been a fraction of what other ex-Communist countries such as Poland have received since the end of the Cold War. A former Socialist country now firmly on the side of the West as a NATO member and a future European Union member in 2004, Poland received about $7 billion in foreign financial assistance in 2001 when Russia received about $1 billion.[56] The war on terrorist groups in Afghanistan has provided an opportunity for the United States to expand its political and military influence in the proximity of Russia as a means for its "containment."

Finally, the United States has an economic/strategic interest in Afghanistan because of its geographical situation. As mentioned earlier, as part of the Pakistani route, this country could offer a route for oil and gas exports of the landlocked Caspian countries. In the Taliban era, the civil war made use of the route out of the question. However, the end of the civil war has revived the old plan. Afghanistan is still far from being stable and may not be so in the near future. Nevertheless, the idea of a gas pipeline from Turkmenistan to Pakistan via Afghanistan abandoned in 1999 has reemerged in the post–Taliban era. In May 2002, Turkmenistan, Pakistan, and Afghanistan signed a trilateral agreement for the construction of a gas pipeline.[57] The agreement reflected the American plan of bypassing Iran and Russia for Turkmen gas exports. Owing to a growing disagreement between the Americans and the Russians over regional and international issues and the persistence of hostile relations between the Americans and the Iranians, the use of an alternative long-term route to those of Iran and Russia has become even more important for the United States. Currently, the entire Turkmen natural gas exports are conducted through the Russian pipeline network, excluding a small amount exported to Iran through a 200-kilometer pipeline. This pipeline which connects Turkmenistan's Korpedzhe gas field with Iran's Kurd-Kuy, was inaugurated in December 1997.[58] Signed in May 1997, a Turkmen agreement with Iran and Turkey for the export of gas to Turkey and Europe via Iran is yet to be implemented.[59] Beside the mentioned American objective, the 2002 trilateral agreement demonstrated Turkmenistan's interest in exporting its gas through a route out of the existing Russian one. It also reflected the desire of Pakistan to establish itself as a main transit route for Caspian oil and gas exports. This desire now seems to enjoy the backing of the American government also as a reward for Pakistan's taking sides with it in its war in Afghanistan.

NOTES

1. Population Division and Statistics Division of the United Nations Secretariat, 2002. (Internet version)

2. "We Will not Repeat the Mistake We Made with the Afghan Refugees," *Ettela'at Binolmelali* (Tehran), 7 August 2002, 2.

3. "Illegal Migration of Afghans to Iran Has Resumed," *Ettela'at Binolmelali* (Tehran), 8 August 2002, 2.

4. United Nations High Commissioner for Refugees (UNHCR), 10 September 2002.

5. UNSCN, "Asia—Selected Situations: Afghanistan Region," *RNIS* 39, October 2002, 47.

6. The World Bank, Statistics, 17 April 2003. (Internet version)

7. Ibid.

8. Ibid.

9. The World Bank, quoted in Afghanistan-Country Report, Jane's Information Group, June 2003. (Internet version)

10. Ibid.

11. WHO-UNICEF. Statistics, 2002. (Internet version)

12. FAO/WFP, Crop and Food Supply Assessment for 2002/2003, 16 August 2002.

13. For information on the 1978 coup, see: Geoffrey Hosking, *A History of the Soviet Union* (London: Fontana Paperbacks and William Collins, 1985), 456–459.

14. For an account on factors that contributed to the creation of the Taliban, see: Burchard Brentjes and Helga Brentjes, *Taliban: A Shadow Over Afghanistan* (Varanasi, India: Rishi Publications, 2002).

15. For views on the social roots of the Taliban, see: Ibid.; see also, Neamatollah Nojumi, *The Rise of the Taliban in Afghanistan: Mass Mobilization, Civil War, and the Future of the Region* (London: Palgrave Macmillan, 2001).

16. Regarding the role of exporting oil from Central Asia in the creation of the Taliban, see: Chapter 1: Petroleum and War Again, in *Taliban;* see also, Ahmed Rashid, *Taliban: Islam, Oil and the New Great Game in Central Asia* (London: I. B. Tauris, May 2002).

17. News, Radio of the Islamic Republic of Iran, 14 October 2002.

18. Hooman Peimani, "Drug-Trafficking in the Ferghana Valley and Instability in Central Asia," *The Times of Central Asia* (Bishkek), 2 November 2000, 4.

19. "Iranian Representative: We Spend 400 Million Dollars Annually to Combat Drug-Trafficking," *Ettela'at Binolmelali* (Tehran), 16 March 1998, 2.

20. Tamara Makarenko, "Compromised from the Start: The Afghan Interim Administration and the Drugs Trade," *Central Asia—Caucasus Analyst* (Baltimore), 31 July 2002.

21. News, Radio of the Islamic Republic of Iran, 14 October 2002.

22. For an account on President Gorbachev's foreign policy, see: Paul Marantz, *From Lenin to Gorbachev: Changing Soviet Perspectives on East-West Relations* (Ottawa: Canadian Institute for International Peace and Security, May 1988).

23. Regarding the process of the deterioration of Sino-Soviet relations, see: O. Edmund Clubb, *20th Century China,* 3rd edition (New York: Columbia University Press, 1978), 350–395.

24. Russia, China, Sign Friendship Treaty," Associated Press, July 16, 2001.

25. For additional information on the Sino-Indian war of 1962, see: Ned Maxwell, *India's China War* (London: Jonathan Cape, 1971).

26. Amalendu Misra, "India at 50: Democracy, Nationalism and Foreign Policy Choices," *Asian Affairs,* 30, Part 1 (February 1999): 54.

27. "U.S. Concern: Moscow-Beijing Arms Deals," United Press International (UPI), 30 November 2000. (Accessed via NewsMax.comWires).

28. For additional information on the independence movement in Sinkiang Province since 1991 and its suppression by the Chinese government, see: Hooman Peimani, *Failed Transition, Bleak Future? War and Instability in Central Asia and the Caucasus* (Westport, CT: Praeger, 2002), 79–80.

29. See Amnesty International Reports for 1995–2001, for instance.

30. "Intelligence: Explosive Mission," *Far Eastern Economic Review,* 1 April 1999, 6.

31. Ibid.

32. "Dr. Rohani: Afghanistan Will Not Become Pakistan's Backyard," *Ettela'at Binolmelali* (Tehran), 17 August 1998, 6.

33. Iranian Representative," 2.

34. "Drug Addiction Devastates the Youth," *Abrar* (Tehran), 15 July 2002, 6.

35. For an analysis of Iranian relations with the newly independent states of Central Asia and the Caucasus in the 1990s, see: Hooman Peimani, *Regional Security and the Future of Central Asia: The Compettion of Iran, Turkey, and Russia* (Westport, CT: Praeger, 1998), 30–36, 52–53, 80–84, 106–116.

36. For an account of Iranian-Azeri relations, see: Hooman Peimani, *Iran and the United States: The Rise of the West Asian Regional Grouping* (Westport, CT: Praeger, 1999), 35–38.

37. Amberin Zaman, "Turkey: A Polarized Society," *The Middle East* 222 (April 1993), 25; "Turkey Anti-Terrorism Agreement with Iran," *Keesing's Record of World Events* 39, No. 12 (December 1993), 39790.

38. "July Chronology," *Middle East International* 482 (26 August 1994), 15.

39. For detailed information on Iran's ties with its southern neighbors and their improvement since the election of President Mohammad Khatami, see: Peimani, *Iran and the United States*, 22, 38–42; Hooman Peimani "Bahrain Turns to Iran." *Asia Times online* (Hong Kong), 22 August 2002; Hooman Peimani, "Iran and Kuwait Close Ranks." *Asia Times online* (Hong Kong), 25 September 2002; Hooman Peimani, "The Ties That Bind Iran and Saudi Arabia." *Asia Times online* (Hong Kong), 16 August 2002.

40. Regarding the political, economic, social, and military/security factors making Iran interested in Central Asia, see: Peimani, *Regional Security and the Future of Central Asia,* 52–53, 82–84, 106–111.

41. For an account on the rise and expansion of authoritarianism in Central Asia and the Caucasus, see: Peimani, *Failed Transition, Bleak Future?*

42. For information on Pakistan's efforts to turn itself into a major export route for exporting Caspian oil and gas, see: Hooman Peimani, *Nuclear Proliferation in the Indian Subcontinent: The Self-Exhausting "Superpowers" and Emerging Alliances* (Westport, CT: Praeger, 2000), 29–32; Hooman Peimani, *The Caspian Pipeline Dilemma: Political Games and Economic Losses* (Westport, CT: Praeger, 2001), 74–76.

43. For detailed information on India's nuclear capability, see: Peimani, *Nuclear Proliferation in the Indian Subcontinent,* 7–12, 17–20, 53.

44. Dr. Rohani, 6.

45. Ramtanu Maitra, "Indian Military Showdown over Central Asia," *Asia Times online* (Hong Kong), 10 September 2002.

46. For an account on the Indian and the Pakistani nuclear arsenal and missile capabilities, see: Peimani, *Nuclear Proliferation in the Indian Subcontinent,* 17–21, 53.

47. For detailed information about the North-South Corridor Agreement, see: Hooman Peimani, "Eurasian Transport Link Faces Roadblocks." *Asia Times online* (Hong Kong), 14 June 2002; Sudha Ramachandran, "India, Iran, Russia Map Out Trade Route," *Asia Times online* (Hong Kong), 29 June 2002.

48. Peimani, *Regional Security and the Future of Central Asia,* 71–72.

49. Drug Abuse Prevention, Republic of Belarus, info@nodrug.by, www.correspondent.net, July 28, 2001.

50. Ibid., 117.

51. Peimani, *The Caspian Pipeline Dilemma,* 13, 63–64, 75–76.

52. "Iran's New Agreements on Energy," *Eurasian File* (Ankara), 112 (January 1999): 7.

53. RFE/RL, 24 August 2002.

54. Ibid.

55. The World Bank. *World Development Indicators 2001* (Washington, D.C.: The World Bank, 2001), 44–45; UNDP, *Human Development Report 2001* (New York: Oxford University Press, 2001), 178–179.

56. "Review of Economic Performance in Eastern Europe," *Transition*, June 2002, 18.

57. Aftab Kazi and Tariq Saeedi, "India and the Politics of the Trans-Afghan Gas Pipeline," *Central Asia—Caucasus Analyst* (Baltimore), 28 August 2002. (Internet version)

58. "Pipeline to Transfer Turkmen Gas Via Iran Became Operational," *Ettela'at Binolmelali* (Tehran), 5 January 1998, 12.

59. Peimani, *Regional Security and the Future of Central Asia,* ix.

3

Afghanistan in the Post–Taliban Era

BRIEF ACCOUNT ON THE TALIBAN'S FALL

The Taliban regime fell in November 2001. Given its sudden appearance in 1994 and its rapid expansion in the second half of the 1990s, its swift collapse was totally unpredictable. Without a doubt, the regime lacked a popular basis of support, a major factor in its demise. For its blatant promotion of Pashtun ethnicity, it alienated all other ethnic groups feeling discriminated against by the Pashtuns. In its bid to subjugate other Afghan ethnic groups, it committed grave atrocities, including the massacre of the people of Bamian, Taligan, and Mazar-i-Sharif in 1998. Having secured the hatred of about 60 percent of the Afghans by this policy, its efforts to create a medieval religious society and its implementation of rigid religious laws for all Afghans regardless of their ethnicity ensured the resentment of the overwhelming majority of Afghans, including the Pashtuns. Excluding a degree of popular support in certain Pashtun tribal areas in the south and southeast bordering Pakistan, the Taliban's lack of popular support created ground for their regime's quick fall. In such a situation, the massive American military operation in October and November 2001 made it weak enough to be washed away by the advancing Northern Alliance forces. The Taliban's few-thousand strong military force was unable to resist and remain in power in about 90 percent of Afghanistan where the group was ruling before its removal from power. The inflow of thousands of civilian volunteers from Pakistan's Pashtun areas did not change its fate. Knowing their inability to win a conventional war launched against them by

American and Northern Alliance forces, those Taliban fighters who survived the first few weeks of war retreated to their ethnic areas in the southern part of Afghanistan or across the border in Pakistan's North-West Frontier Province. Based on both rumours and evidence, the Pashtun tribal leaders in both countries provided them and their al-Qaeda ally with shelter and protection, a situation that remained in effect in 2003. After about a year, the remnants of the Taliban and al-Qaeda forces began conducting small-scale hit-and-run operations against the Afghan and American military, a sign of their regrouping after a long period of inability to offer any resistance.

SITUATION IN THE POST–TALIBAN ERA

The fall of the Taliban regime in November 2001 did not only end seven years of fear and atrocity, but also ended the two-decade Afghan civil war. That war pitted against each other various Afghan groups of different ideological commitments, political persuasions, religious convictions, and ethnicity. This sudden development was an absolute prerequisite for ending chaos and lawlessness caused by a lack of central government in full control of the entire country. In turn, the establishment of a fully-functional central government was a necessity for addressing the phenomenal devastation of the country after over two decades of war. Thus, the end of civil war created a hope for the beginning of a new era in the history of the war-torn country, an era of peace and construction. However, the history of Afghanistan since November 2001 has shown various signs of possible troubles ahead, which could plunge the country once again into an unpredictable period of instability. This is notwithstanding the positive developments in the post–Taliban era, such as an end to rampant state-sponsored abuses of human rights and the opening of previously-banned schools for girls in many cities. The following account of major characteristics, developments, and trends, as well as the principal concerns and objectives of the powers with an interest in Afghanistan, should shed light on the situation since the removal of the Taliban from power.

MAJOR CHARACTERISTICS

The post–Taliban era has certain characteristics that create grounds for concern both in Afghanistan and elsewhere. Such characteristics could neutralize all efforts on the part of those who have contributed to the Taliban's fall, Afghan political forces and the regional and nonregional states alike. As well, those characteristics could hamper their efforts to stabilize Afghanistan and to create a viable political system for the war-torn country in need of a strong central government. Unless the major sources of concern are addressed, Afghanistan will most probably find itself in another round of instability in the form of a civil war with all its associated evils as experienced for over two decades.

To establish a broad-based and widely-acceptable Afghan government, the Taliban's disappearance from the political scene and the international community's interest in the stability of Afghanistan were, and still are, insufficient, although important, factors. For all the interested parties, the main challenge is to create a consensus among the major ethnic and political groups to end the situation conducive to the resumption of civil war and to ensure stability in Afghanistan. All those who have suffered from its instability in one way or another (i.e., the Afghans, their neighbors, and many other nations affected by the drug-trafficking or terrorism rooted in Afghanistan) will benefit from a stable Afghanistan. Yet, the achievement of that objective requires the cooperation of certain states that have backed rival Afghan groups over the last two decades. As a major external factor, over time their pursuit of conflicting interests has contributed to the persistence of ethnic and political strife among the Afghan groups and to the prolongation of civil war. Although it is not in full swing in the post–Taliban era, such a war may reemerge in the near future as its root causes are yet to be addressed. Without such cooperation, the creation of a truly representative and durable Afghan government will be simply an impossible mission.

As a positive development, the Taliban's fall prepared grounds for the establishment of a central government in Afghanistan when the interest of the international community in that country's stability matched the desire of the Afghans to end their prolonged lawlessness. Sponsored by those interested in a stable Afghanistan, the Bonn conference of December 2001 aimed at laying the foundation of an Afghan central government. During the conference, negotiations among different Afghan groups representing the diverse ethnic and religious makeup of the country did not solve all the grievances, conflicts, and hostilities among and between different Afghan groups, which had fueled their hostility for a long time. Given the existence of old and deep-rooted conflicts and ethnic rivalry, those negotiations only created a minimum consensus among the participants. The latter was necessary for the creation of a provisional government as a first step toward building a future consensus for the foundation of a permanent political system led by a fully functional central government. To achieve its very limited objective, the Bonn agreement left many major issues unresolved, which left room for the rise of a variety of problems in the post–Taliban era. They include ethnic conflicts, the reemergence of warlords, international drug-trafficking, and severe economic problems. While being separate issues, they are all interrelated reflecting different dimensions of the unresolved problems.

Ethnic Conflicts

The Bonn agreement was reached under certain circumstances. The sudden change in the political situation in Afghanistan (i.e., the fall of the Taliban and the rise of the Northern Alliance) created an extraordinary situation.

Overwhelmingly Pashtun in ethnicity, the demise of the Taliban brought about the lowering status of the Pashtuns as an ethnic group throughout Afghanistan. There were two major reasons for this development. First, this was a "natural" phenomenon given the atrocities committed by the Taliban all over the country, especially against non-Pashtuns. Of course, the Taliban did not enjoy the unconditional support of all Pashtuns. Nevertheless, their clear efforts to suppress other ethnic groups and to monopolize the political power for their own ethnic group created a strong anti-Pashtun sentiment in Afghanistan. This was notwithstanding the fact that their harsh religious laws targeted all Afghans regardless of their ethnicity. Added to this, the absence of any Pashtun-based anti-Taliban group resulting from a tacit consensus reached between the Taliban and Afghanistan's Pashtun tribes contributed to the anti-Pashtun sentiment. The fact that the only significant anti-Taliban force was the Northern Alliance, a coalition of non-Pashtun groups dominated by the Tajiks, reinforced this sentiment. The latter also weakened the case for a larger share of the power for the Pashtuns in the post–Taliban government. In the end, the only force that had the capability to topple the Taliban with the assistance of the regional powers (mainly Iran and Russia) and the direct military backing of a nonregional power (the United States) was the Northern Alliance. The limited fighting of some Pashtun tribes against the Taliban in their last days was too insignificant and too late to change their role in Afghan politics. Such activity was mainly the result of appreciating the emerging political reality characterized by the falling fortune of the Taliban; the changing political tide justified their changing sides. As well, their limited fighting reflected their efforts to ensure the control of the Pashtun territories by themselves in a bid to stop the seemingly unstoppable southward expansion of the Northern Alliance. The Northern Alliance's military capability and its years of fighting against the Taliban granted it both the physical means and the legitimacy to dominate the post–Taliban political system, a development welcomed by the majority of Afghans and many regional and nonregional states.

Second, a lowering of status of the Pashtuns was also a natural reflection of a demographic change in the Afghan society upsetting the ethnic balance in favor of the non-Pashtuns. As the Taliban's fall changed the political scene overnight, the new political reality enabled the non-Pashtun ethnic groups to claim a superior status after centuries of social and political inferiority. This reality helped them to capitalize on their demographic strength requiring a corresponding political status. Given the military and political weaknesses of the Pashtuns, others could actually receive a share of the power even far larger than their demographic share of about 60 percent.

Against this background, there was not any surprise that the Pashtuns did not get a significant share of the post–Taliban government. Of course, Hamid Karzai, a Pashtun, was appointed the head of the transitional government named the Interim Government. However, by no means did this indicate a change of mood in favor of the Pashtuns. The pressure exercised by the Americans, the appreciation by the Northern Alliance of a need to create a national reconciliation government, and the consent of the regional powers (Iran, Pakistan, and Russia) made his appointment feasible. However, the inclusion of Pashtuns in the government and their appointment at the provincial level did not satisfy their expectations. This is, however, only partly because of the natural backlash of the Taliban era on the appointment process. As mentioned before, the Pashtuns have been the dominant political force in Afghanistan for the last few centuries. They have nearly monopolized the Afghan government and the military under various political systems whether monarchy or republic, a situation that prevailed under the atheist Afghan Communists and the ultra-religious Taliban, alike. For this reason, the Pashtuns are not prepared to settle for anything less than their traditional status, although they account for only about 40 percent of the population, a nondisputable demographic fact.

In such a situation, the fact that the Northern Alliance is supported by other Afghan ethnic groups accounting for about 60 percent of the population has had no bearing on the Pashtuns' expectations. No wonder if they are dissatisfied with the post–Taliban era, by and large. Thus, the Pashtun chieftains have expressed their unhappiness with the status quo by refusing to accept the authority of the central government. The following recent example sheds light on the argument. In early September 2002, Commander of American forces in Afghanistan Lieutenant General Dan McNeill met with Pasha Khan Zadran, an anti-government Pashtun warlord operating near the town of Khost in the Paktia province.[1] Facing the obstacles created by the warlord opposed to the Kabul government, the purpose of his meeting was to discuss "ways to improve the mobility of coalition forces."[2] While collaborating with the American forces, the warlord opposed the Afghan transitional government because of President Karzai's appointment of a new governor for Khost—Mr. Hakim Taniwal.

This ethnic strife is also reflected in the eruption of anti-Pashtun sentiment in the non-Pashtun areas formerly under the Taliban control. The grave atrocities committed by the Taliban against non-Pashtuns in those areas created a very strong anti-Pashtun sentiment in especially the northern part of the country inhabited by mainly Uzbeks and Tajiks. According to a United Nations spokesperson in Afghanistan in October 2002, "thousands of Pashtuns" faced harassment and displacement in the northern part of Afghanistan dominated by non-Pashtuns in the post–Taliban era.[3] The military forces loyal to non-Pashtun warlords have reportedly committed atrocities against the Pashtun minority in their regions. As a recent example, in October 2002 forces loyal to Uzbek warlord and Deputy Defence Minister Abdulrashid Dostum forced hundreds of ethnic Pashtuns to leave four villages in the Pir Naqshi region of northern Afghanistan, a region controlled by the forces of another warlord, Ahmad Khan.[4] Based on interviews conducted by humanitarian workers in that region, some of the Pashtun women involved in the case claimed to have been raped, while others claimed that their homes had been looted.[5]

Reemergence of Warlords

A major characteristic of the post–Taliban era has been the rise of warlords. Prior to the emergence of the Taliban, the absence of a fully functional central government made the situation ripe for the rise of warlords who controlled their receptive regions as independent rulers. In its bid to expand its control to the entire country, the Taliban suppressed the warlords or forced them to submit to their authority in the areas under their control, accounting for about 90 percent of the country when their regime collapsed. In the remaining areas, fear of being overrun by the Taliban who seemed unstoppable forced the Uzbek, Tajik, and Hazara warlords to accept temporarily cooperation in their areas, by and large. The Taliban's fall relieved the pressure from the warlords in different regions, especially in the southern parts formerly firmly under the Taliban. Seen by them as their rightful realms, the aspiration of the warlords to exercise power in their respective territories for all the economic and noneconomic benefits created a strong temptation once the barrier to their rule was out of the way. Also, in the absence of a strong central government, the need for running local affairs required the filling of the political vacuum. The warlords took the opportunity without any hesitation.

Additional factors are responsible for the re-rise of warlords all over the country. One factor has been the pursuit of national interests of certain powers. In particular, in its fight against the remnants of the Taliban and al-Qaeda, the American government has sought to mobilize in Afghanistan all forces that could help it achieve its objective. This situation has resulted in assisting those warlords willing to fight alongside the American forces, mainly in the Pashtun areas where the Taliban have some popular backing. The warlords' power has strengthened in their region at the expense of weakening that of the Afghan central government. This is an unintentional consequence of an American policy damaging another American objective in Afghanistan, that of establishing a strong central government to end decades of instability as a bedrock of terrorism. Famous warlords who have taken sides with the American forces and who have been involved in bloody turf wars in the north and southern parts of Afghanistan include Tajik warlord General Atta Mohammed (also known as Ustad Atta), Uzbek warlord General Abdulrashid Dostum, and Pashtun warlord Pasha Khan Zardan. As will be discussed, the last one has been an ally of the American forces in Pashtun-dominated Khost Province in command of a force of 6,000, which outnumbers that of the Khost governor of about 600.[6]

Fear of ill treatment by a government dominated by a hostile ethnic group has created a popular ground in Afghanistan in favor of local governments run by warlords who are from the same ethnic groups as their respective local populations. As a result, the Pashtun region has become suitable for the rise of warlords and their rivalry. The domination of the Afghan central government by non-Pashtuns and their sudden increased military power have created concern among the Pashtuns. Their warlords who have resisted the central government to keep their respective regions under their own control are now seen, at least by a significant number of Pashtuns, as acting in their best interests. In this regard, the case of Pasha Khan Zardan has been very famous. Demanding the position of governorship of his home Province of Khost located in the southeastern part of Afghanistan, he has refused to accept the authority of the central government and its appointed governor since its formation in December 2001.[7] A dominant force in Khost, he has forced the Kabul-appointed governor (Hakim Taniwal) to operate from a guesthouse as Mr. Zardan has settled himself in the governor's office.[8]

The reemergence of warlords has had major negative consequences for the devastated Afghanistan. Beside its contributions to drug-trafficking, it has negatively affected the process of government creation in Afghanistan. The reappearance of warlords on the political scene has created grounds for an inevitable rivalry between and among them. Seeking to consolidate their power over their territories and/or to expand their control over areas run by other warlords, they have resorted to bloody wars to achieve their objectives. Undoubtedly, the latter has contributed both to lawlessness and absence of safety for the average Afghans. Territorial wars between warlords have become a frequent phenomenon in the post–Taliban era. For example during the first half of 2002, the outbreak of a bloody turf war between warlords in April and May left thirty-one people dead and another eighty-five wounded in two regions of Afghanistan.[9] In the north, forces loyal to Uzbek warlord General Abdulrashid Dostum and Tajik warlord General Atta Mohammed clashed over controlling two towns near the city of Mazar-i-Sharif, namely Sare Pul and Shulgara. In the east, two Pashtun warlords, Pasha Khan Zardan and Taj Mohammed Wardak, fought over the city of Gardez. In the second half of 2002, many territorial wars between warlords also occurred. For example, in August, in the north, fighting erupted between the Tajik fighters loyal to General Atta Mohammed, an ally of Defence Minister General Mohammad Fahim and a member of his faction (Jamat-i Islami), and Uzbek fighters loyal to General Abdulrashid Dostum, a vice minister of defence.[10] In the same month, in the district of Kahmad to the northwest of the Shiite-dominated city of Bamiyan, fighting took place between the local battalion commander, Rahmatullah, and the forces of General Tufan.[11] The fighting over the control of their region took place despite their official alignment with the Afghan ministry of defense.

International Drug-Trafficking

The reemergnce of the warlords has contributed to the expansion of Afghanistan-based international drug-trafficking. In order to maintain their privileges, the warlords have every reason to remain independent despite the Afghan interim government's efforts to the contrary. Such a situation hints at the persistence of a suitable ground for Afghanistan-based international drug-trafficking, which has been the warlords' major source of income since the 1980s. Without a doubt, the operation of this destructive "industry" will have security implications for Afghanistan and its neighboring states. Furthermore, it will have a negative impact on inter- and intra-ethnic rivalry, on the consolidation of the Afghan central government, and on the reconstruction of its devastated country.

The post–Taliban era has created grounds for the expansion both of drug production and trafficking. The opium and heroin production in Afghanistan and Afghanistan-based international drug-trafficking are a by-product of over two decades of chaos, lawlessness, and poverty caused and reinforced by a civil war that lasted until the Taliban's fall. That development removed a major obstacle to ending the Afghan civil war, but it did not eliminate four major contributing factors to the operation of the drug "industry": rampant poverty, lack of a viable economy, ethnic rivalry, and the absence of a strong central government. The first two factors have motivated many Afghan peasants to substitute nonprofitable traditional farming (e.g., grain and fruit production) with financially rewarding opium production, while creating a large army of recruits for drug-trafficking. The interim Afghan government's program to motivate farmers to substitute their opium poppy cultivation with other crops by paying them for the destruction of their poppy crop is yet to be fully implemented.

On the one hand, this is a result of a lack of adequate funds created by the international community's reluctance to fund that program fully. Consequently, late in 2002, there were reportedly many farmers who were yet to be paid for giving up their opium crop late in 2001 when the program was initiated.[12] On the other hand, this is an outcome of the insignificance of the amount offered to the opium-producing farmers. Glenn Mitterman of the United Nations Office for Drug Control and Crime Prevention (UNDCP) in Kabul stressed this point in April 2002, although he welcomed the interim government's offer of $250 per destroyed opium field. According to him, "U.S. $250 per 2,000 [square meters of poppy] field is way below what farmers will get from selling their opium crop."[13] He added the necessity of other initiatives to complement the payment projects by creating further incentives for opium farmers as he geared the success of the program to the opium farmers' seeing "something tangible happening, like the construction of roads and schools."[14] Owing to the absence of adequate international development funds for Afghanistan, the progress in those areas is still very insignificant. No wonder if the overwhelming majority of the Afghan farmers involved in the opium poppy production have yet to show any interest in the program.

Apart from foreign influences, the other two contributing factors to the drug "industry," ethnic rivalry and the absence of a strong central government, have given birth to warlords. Having ruled over their respective ethnic territories as independent rulers for over two decades, the bloody rivalry among the warlords has prolonged ethnic conflicts while preventing the formation of a fully functional central government. In turn, this situation has denied reconstruction in Afghanistan. In the absence of a strong central government in control of the entire country, the prevailing lawlessness and the impoverishment of Afghanistan have created suitable conditions for the production and trafficking of narcotics under protection of the local warlords. Drug-generated income and hard currency have been the main domestic source of revenue for almost all the major Afghan political actors over the last two decades, the warlords and the Taliban alike. The latter turned Afghanistan into the largest global producer of opium and heroin. In 1999, the opium production reached the phenomenal level of 4,600 tons.[15] The Taliban regime also created a safe haven for international drug-traffickers, but its fall did not change the situation. The drug "industry" has continued to grow. Under severe international pressure, the Taliban regime imposed a partial ban on opium production only to disappear in the post–Taliban era despite the Afghan interim government's commitment to fight the drug "industry."

Apart from the rampant poverty and lack of employment opportunity, the weakness of the Afghan central government has enabled the continuation of the drug "industry." The majority of warlords have accepted the authority of the Afghan interim government in words, while governing their territories as independent rulers in practice. In the absence of any major international effort to revitalize Afghanistan's economy, the emerging disagreements among the warlords over their share of power and their respective ethnic groups' role in the future of Afghanistan have prepared grounds for inter- and intra-ethnic fighting. In particular, this has been evident in the Pashtun-dominated east and southeast Afghanistan where most of the opium, the main ingredient of heroin, is cultivated. The Afghan interim government simply lacks any power outside Kabul, including in the regions where opium is cultivated, to enforce its ban. Reports suggest a significant increase in opium production and its future continuity despite the interim government's ban on opium cultivation. In the absence of any Afghan government official statistics, all estimates indicate a sudden large increase in opium production in 2002. In August of that year, the United Nations estimated the opium production for the entire year to be at least 2,952 tons.[16] According to a report presented in September 2002 at an international drug-trafficking conference in Paris, opium cultivation in Afghanistan rose at least by 2,000 tons compared to 2001.[17] The report estimated the total opium yield for 2002 to be up to 2,700 tons.[18] However, in October 2002 Ali Hashemi, Iran's commander of the anti-narcotic unit, estimated the opium production for 2002 at between 3,500 and 4,000 tons.[19] Western intelligence estimates are closer to the Iranian one as they suggest that the 2002 harvest could have produced 4,500 tons of opium or 450 tons of heroin.[20]

In short, a year after the Taliban's fall, Afghanistan reclaimed its status as the largest producer of opium. That country lost that status to the Golden Triangle in Thailand, Laos, and Myanmar when the Taliban sharply reduced opium production in 2001. The Golden Triangle was estimated to produce about 900 tons of opium in 2002.[21]

As evident in the huge increase in opium production, the Afghan government's ban has been ignored by the local warlords who, like their people, have no other reliable source of income. Being involved in a fierce territorial war with both Pashtun and non-Pashtun warlords, the Pashtun warlords controlling most of the opium producing regions have expressed dissatisfaction over their share of power in the interim government. Since January 2002, fights over controlling territories between and among warlords and between them and certain warlords who now function as government-appointed regional authorities have been a common occurrence in the Pashtun regions. In late April 2002, Pasha Khan Zardan's firing rockets into the eastern city of Gardez controlled by Gardez governor Taj Mohammed Wardak was just a recent example of this trend.[22]

The Afghan drug "industry" will continue as long as Afghanistan suffers from two major deficiencies: the absence of a strong central government, and the lack of a viable economy capable of generating enough revenue for the government and adequate numbers of well-paid jobs for the people. Facing a wide range of immediate problems, the interim government, whose power is confined only to Kabul, lacks resources to contain the warlords and to prevent opium farming and the production of opium and heroin. Out of force, it has de facto accepted as tragic realities the authority of the warlords, their destructive territorial and ethnic wars, and their drug related activities, including allowing drug production and harboring international drug-traffickers. This "acceptance" is notwithstanding the destructive impact of those realities on its power and on peace and stability in Afghanistan, which are the prerequisites for any meaningful reconstruction project. The latter will be simply out of the question so long as this situation persists.

The Afghan central government's weakness enables warlords to operate as independent territorial rulers who allow the production and the trafficking of drugs. In the absence of other reliable sources of employment and income, this is a means of employment for their people and a reliable source of income for their local political and military apparatus. In turn, this situation weakens the power of the government and contributes to lawlessness, which prolong economic paralysis and its resulting poverty. These factors guarantee the continuation of the drug "industry." The warlords' hefty shares of this operation enable them to consolidate their position as independent local rulers at the central government's expense.

There is no realistic basis for the success of the interim government and its successor in addressing the deficiencies that create grounds for the production and trafficking of drugs in the foreseeable future. This is due to certain parameters, including the strength of the warlords, Afghanistan's impoverishment, and the half-hearted commitment of the international community to Afghanistan's economic development. Therefore, Afghanistan will remain the largest global producer of opium and heroin and a center for international drug-trafficking for an unpredictable period of time. Apart from its obvious health hazards, Afghanistan-based drug-trafficking and its related crimes will be a destabilizing factor not only for Afghanistan, but also for all the countries on the trafficking route: Iran, Turkey, Russia, and the Central Asian and Caucasian countries. Such an operation will be also a major contributing factor to the warlords' strength and to their inter- and intra-ethnic turf wars with a negative impact on the consolidation of the Afghan central government and on the Afghan economy's revitalization.

Severe Economic Problems

When it comes to the economy, post–Taliban Afghanistan is not fundamentally different from the Taliban era. In practice, the country lacks any functioning economy to speak of, due to its severe underdevelopment and devastating civil war. As was the case under the Taliban regime, there are serious obstacles to the existence of a functioning economy and to normal economic activities for which at least four major factors are responsible.

First, Afghanistan lacks stability. This is the absolute necessity for conducting durable, profitable, and productive economic activities, in general, and for embarking on any economic development program, in particular. Stability demands a fully functional government in control of the entire country, an objective yet to be achieved. So long as instability persists in one form or another, the fear of resumption of a fully-fledged civil war or chaos and lawlessness create disincentive on the part of foreign donors and investors and also the Afghans to embark on any major economic project. A politically stable, peaceful, and predictable society is an absolute prerequisite for the creation of a viable economy for Afghanistan, which, in turn, is a must for its political stability.

Second, the country lacks adequate domestic sources of financing for any development or reconstruction project. In fact, it lacks the very basic financial means to meet the salaries of its small numbers of civil servants and military and law enforcement personnel. As reported in October 2002, many government employees, police officers, and military personnel were not paid for several months, and that, out of desperation, many of them resorted to robbery and looting in 2002.[23] The foreign donors so far have provided the very basics, but it is not certain for how long they will continue to do so. Because of its heavy cost, there is a fear backed by the realties that the latter will not be very keen on assisting the country to address its fundamental problems, including its lack of infrastructure, a prerequisite for any serious long-term development project. The Tokyo conference in early 2002 gathered many regional and nonregional donors who pledged to provide about $5 billion to finance the necessary economic reconstruction of the country as a necessity for ensuring its stability and its return to normalcy. Evidence indicates that most of the pledged financial assistance packages will not be honored. By late 2002, this has been evident in a very limited actual transfer of funds by the donors to the Afghan government equal to less than 20 percent of the promised amount. Of the transferred amount, most of the funds seem to have been spent not on helping Afghanistan deal with its development problems, but on non-Afghan organizations mandated to help the Afghans. In his October 2002 speech at the annual meeting of the Economic Cooperation Organization (ECO) in Istanbul, Afghan President Hamid Karzai referred to that problem. Accordingly, he described "how upset he was to hear earlier this year that $890 million had been spent on aid in Afghanistan, but that $800 million of it had gone to the UN and other aid agencies."[24]

Third, Afghanistan lacks the minimum infrastructure necessary for any significant type of economic activity. In fact, the country lacks even the infrastructure to meet the basic needs of the population in the fields of education, health, transportation, energy, and water, to name a few. The absence of the basic infrastructure creates a major barrier to economic activities, including major developmental projects, apart from its grave consequences for the population at large.

Finally, Afghanistan lacks an adequate number of trained workforce, whether skilled workers or professionals. On the one hand, this is the result of the inability of its small and underdeveloped educational system to train the needed workforce. This economic handicap was worsened significantly by the Taliban regime as it closed down many educational institutions and marginalized the educated people. On the other hand, this is an outcome of the migration by force or choice of the overwhelming majority of the educated Afghans to Western and regional countries. There is no realistic hope for their voluntary return to Afghanistan to help build their country in the foreseeable future. This is the result of certain factors, including their establishment of various social attachments to their new home countries, the uncertain future of their motherland, and the lack of attractive employment or investment opportunities there. As a result, for a predictably long time, foreign countries with an interest in the stability of Afghanistan will likely have to bear the heavy burden of providing the educated cadre for the reconstruction of that country.

The poor economic situation is a major problem in the post–Taliban era. Its resulting evils such as poverty, malnutrition, and extensive unemployment contribute to the prolongation of the status quo, which is prone to instability in various forms, including civil war.

MAJOR TRENDS IN THE POST–TALIBAN ERA

The fall of the Taliban regime ended years of devastating civil war and pushed Afghanistan into a new era. Despite their differences, all the Afghans have since hoped that this new era will bring about durable peace and political certainty, although the rival Afghan groups have different views about how to create a new Afghanistan and under whom. The disappearance of the Taliban as a major political and military force, the Afghans' desire to end the civil war, and the interest of the international community in peace and stability in Afghanistan have all created grounds for the formation of a stable Afghan government. Despite its uncertain fate, the establishment of an interim government has increased hopes for the achievement of the Afghans' objectives. However, the future of Afghanistan is far from certain, despite the existing positive environment both inside the country and abroad.

In fact, in the post–Taliban era, there are two opposite trends that could determine the fate of Afghanistan under different circumstances. One is a trend toward the creation of a united country run by a single central government acceptable to all the four major ethnic groups and their leaders. This trend reflects the desire of the Afghans for peace and stability after over two decades of war, which turned their country into rubble. As an expression of the popular mood, it has created an essential domestic condition for a nation-building program to overcome chaos and lawlessness requiring a fully functional government. While essential, it is still an insufficient condition to ensure a future for Afghanistan different from its catastrophic past and its uncertain present. It takes a wide range of internal and external conditions to create a cooperative and constructive mood inside the country and in all those regional and nonregional states of significance to its future to make this the dominant trend. Particularly, there is a need for a radical change in its economic situation to generate employment and income for the Afghans in order to create for them not only hope, but also material means to meet their needs. This is a necessity to incline them to rally around their central government full-heartedly. Otherwise, hunger, malnutrition, poverty, and unemployment will diminish, if not totally eliminate, incentives on the part of the Afghans to cooperate with the emerging government. It is a government with little financial means to embark on any project to change the dissatisfactory situation in a short period of time. A weak government incapable of addressing its people's basic needs in education, health, nutrition, and housing will push the Afghans to rally around their local warlords, whether they like it or not. In consequence, such a government will pave the way for the rise and consolidation of local warlords who will seek to perform some of those tasks to whatever extent they can, while providing a degree of security and certainty for their respective citizens. As stated before, the rise and consolidation of the warlords will guarantee the expansion of all the evils of the civil war era, including proxy war and drug-trafficking, only to prepare grounds for the resumption of civil war itself.

The other trend in the post–Taliban era is the one toward ethnic and religious conflicts and the resumption of civil war. With certainty, that will make the country unstable for an unpredictable period of time. The Taliban's fall was a prerequisite for the stabilization of Afghanistan as it removed the barrier to ending the devastating civil war that pitted Afghans against each other. However, it was not the only prerequisite for restoring normalcy to Afghanistan. As a matter of fact, the absence of many other necessary economic and political factors for restoring peace and order to the war-torn country has contributed to a situation containing all the ingredients to put the country back on the path of chaos and instability. If the current dismal economic and social situation persists, there is little doubt, if any at all, that this will be the dominant trend, guaranteeing an indefinite period of agony for the impoverished and devastated Afghans.

The persistence of various factors has prepared grounds for chaos and quite possibly a new round of civil war along ethnic lines. The interim government of Afghanistan, which will stay in power until June 2004, has proven unable to tackle a variety of challenges facing the country. It is too weak politically, economically, financially, and militarily to change the situation for the better. Given these weaknesses, there is no wonder it has little authority outside Kabul. More than that, it is even too weak to preserve its authority in the capital, as reflected in the assassination of its top officials and attempts at President Karzai's life. In February 2002, Afghan Minister for Air Transport and Tourism Abdul Rahman was beaten to death at Kabul airport, while in July 2002, Haji Abdul Qadir, one of President Karzai's three vice-presidents, was assassinated in Kabul.[25] On 5 August 2002, while visiting Pashtun-dominated Kandahar, President Karzai, a Pashtun himself, became the target of an unsuccessful assassination attempt.[26] In July 2002, the replacing of President Karzai's Afghan bodyguards and presidential guards with American military personnel, only to be replaced by U.S. State Department security personnel a month later, who subsequently handed over their duty to an American private security company reflected the depth of the Afghan central government's weakness.[27] There were two major reasons for the move: the inability of the Afghan government's security forces to ensure the security of the top officials, and a strong suspicion about the involvement of those forces in the assassinations. Although an imperative dictated by the circumstances, the replacement has been a source of embarrassment for the president and also for his government, now seen as American puppets.

MAJOR CONCERNS OF THE REGIONAL AND NONREGIONAL POWERS

Despite their regional and international significance, the recent developments in Afghanistan have not significantly changed the long-term objectives of foreign powers with an interest in that country. Competition among major regional and nonregional powers arising from their pursuit of national interests has been a major external factor in intensifying conflicts among various Afghan political groups over the last two decades. For its adding fuel to extensive ethnic and religious conflicts, this has been a major hurdle in the way of establishing a central government representative of and acceptable to the majority of the Afghans. The fall of the Taliban created grounds for a new set of rivalry in that country, as that development suddenly changed the domestic balance of power.

In the post–Taliban era, all the regional and nonregional powers appreciate the importance of a strong central government as an absolute necessity for stability in that country. Its instability will have a negative impact on their countries, of course to a varying extent and in different forms, as it has had since 1978. However, pursuit of their foreign policies has had, and will continue to have, certain effects on the stabilization process as their conflicting interests in cases offset efforts to ensure stability. Their policies toward Afghanistan arise from their fears and concerns related directly to preserving their national interests in Afghanistan and its surrounding regions. So far, none of them has sought to contribute to instability in that country. Depending on the case, their reasons for doing so include one or all of the following. They have an interest in a stable Afghanistan for its impact on their national security. They are interested in the uprooting of the terrorist groups based in Afghanistan, and in using it as a base or a springboard to achieve certain strategic objectives. Finally, they hope to receive a share of its future development projects.

Apart from those incentives, certain factors make the regional and nonregional powers with stakes in Afghanistan cautious in their approach to that country lest their behavior could provoke an international reaction more than they bargain for. The major ones are the uncertainty about the political direction of Afghanistan, concerns about the American military presence there, and the existing international interest in political developments in Afghanistan. The United States apart, fear of being labeled as sabotaging efforts to stabilize Afghanistan and thus knowingly or unknowingly damaging efforts to uproot Afghanistan-based terrorists have created another reason for them not to embark on any major plan for the country at least for awhile.

Thanks to the rapidly changing political environment, the creation of a new government has become a feasible scenario. While changing the political scene in Afghanistan, the new environment has not changed the major objectives, interests, and concerns of the states with stakes in that country. Not surprisingly, they all have sought to influence the ongoing government-making process in their favor. This is due to the fact that the nature of the future Afghan government and its attitude toward its neighboring countries and regions will be important both to their national security and to their political and economic interests. Given this situation, the stake is high for especially Pakistan, the United States, Iran, and Russia. They all appreciate the necessity of a broad-based Afghan government with proportional representation for all Afghan ethnic groups as a prerequisite for peace and stability in Afghanistan and its adjacent region. However, in practice, they also have the incentive to help create a government in which their Afghan allies dominate. The history of the last two decades has created grounds for their concern about the domination of one or another ethnic group that could endanger their national interests to a varying extent.

Major common long-term interests have made Pakistan and the United States natural allies in their approach to Afghanistan in the post–Taliban era. Pakistan has lost its preeminent status in Afghanistan because of the fall of its protégé, namely the Taliban. That development has sharply reduced its leverage in influencing the pace of events in that country. Consequently, it is left with little asset in playing a significant role in the formation of the Afghan government to secure its interests. In fact, Pakistan is now concerned about the growth of influence of Iran, India, and Russia in Afghanistan at its expense, a by-product of the creation of a Northern Alliance-dominated Afghan government. As a sign of compromise, in June 2002 the assembly of elders and tribal leaders tasked with the creation of a provisional government to run the country until 2004 (Loya Jirga), included more Pashtuns in the Afghan government. However, that inclusion has not allayed the fear of the Pakistanis. As the Pashtuns form the main social basis of support for Pakistan, that development will not likely have a major impact on the status quo to address Pakistan's concern. There is a simple reason for this situation. The Pashtuns are not united and lack a unified strong military force capable of matching that of the Northern Alliance. Moreover, many of them view Mr. Karzai not as their representative, but more as a sell-out for his working with a Tajik-dominated government. In such a situation, their political representatives in the government will not have strong clout to influence the situation the way the Pakistanis did in the Taliban era.

For its weak position, Pakistan has found strong reasons to take sides with the United States. Thanks to its military presence in Afghanistan, the latter can play a role in the formation of a future permanent Afghan government. Given the Iranian and Russian historical and military ties with Afghanistan and their strong relations with the Northern Alliance, that role is still limited in comparison to that of Iran and Russia. Of course, the situation could change if the Americans accompanied their military influence in that country with a strong economic presence to incline the Northern Alliance to rally around them in the long run.

Like the Pakistanis, the Americans are also concerned about the growth of influence of Iran, India, and Russia in Afghanistan and Central Asia. Their influence will be even more alarming for the Americans if an Afghan government with positive attitudes toward those countries emerges. Such a scenario would also deny them the possibility of bypassing Iran and Russia for the long-term export of Central Asian gas and oil via Afghanistan and Pakistan. Although the construction of gas and oil pipelines passing through Afghanistan demands a stable and predictable country yet to be created, the conclusion of an agreement in principle among Turkmenistan, Afghanistan, and Pakistan in May 2002 for the construction of a gas pipeline reflected the American interest in this project.[28] The fact that the American companies are the major developers of Turkmenistan's gas fields leaves no doubt in this regard.

Given this situation, the Americans and the Pakistanis have sought to secure a strong, if not a dominant, position in the Afghan government information through certain Pashtun groups with close ties to Pakistan. While the Northern Alliance, Iran, and Russia recognize the necessity of the Pashtun representation in the government, the insistence of the Americans and the Pakistanis on giving a major role to the Pashtuns has reflected their desired type of government. During the Loya Jerga's meeting in June 2002, their push led to the inclusion of more Pashtuns in the government in addition to the reelection of President Hamid Karzai, who will remain in power until the scheduled 2004 elections.[29] A more blatant case has been their raising the idea of the participation of the "moderate" Taliban in the Afghan government, an idea floating around prior to the collapse of the Taliban. Only the sharp objection of Iran and Russia forced them to give it up. Having strong ties with the Pakistani military and being resentful of their loss of traditional dominant political power to the mainly non-Pashtun Northern Alliance, certain Pashtun tribes and groups outside the Northern Alliance are becoming close to Pakistan and the United States. A well-known example is Pasha Khan Zardan, who commands an army of 6,000.[30] He has claims to the governorship of Khost Province bordering Pakistan for his fighting against the Taliban regime in its last days. He was initially appointed governor by the Karzai administration only to be sacked later because of a growing local opposition.[31] The emerging dissatisfaction among the Pashtun warlords could eventually lead to an ethnic war should Mr. Hamid Karzai fail to unite all the Afghans.

If this scenario happens or to avoid its happening, the international peacekeeping force dominated politically and militarily by the Americans and their allies (e.g., British, Canadian, German, and Turkish forces) will likely serve to offset the influence of the Northern Alliance. Moreover, it could function to force it to accept major compromises in the formation of the Afghan government, such as giving a major share of power to the pro-American and pro-Pakistani Pashtun forces. This share could also be secured through linking any major Western aid program for Afghanistan to the existence of such a compromise. However, if Pakistan and the United States continue their so-called pro-Pashtun policy, there is no doubt that Iran, India, and Russia will join forces to secure a dominant position for the Northern Alliance in the future Afghan government. Most probably, the result will be a delay in the creation of a durable Afghan government, if not the beginning of another round of civil war.

Despite their rivalry in the Caucasus and Central Asia and differences over the division of the Caspian Sea among its littoral states, Iran and Russia are friends and allies. Their extensive and multidimensional relations have been growing for over a decade. Those relations are cemented by their common security interests in West Asia, including their opposition to Western (particularly American) influence in that region. This situation has inclined them to work in concert in Afghanistan for the last few years. Not surprisingly, they have a common interest in the formation of an Afghan government with a positive attitude toward them. In a great part, the rapid advancement of the Northern Alliance forces into the south and their control of over 80 percent of Afghanistan in the post–Taliban era have been the results of an Iranian-Russian massive military assistance. The entry of these forces into Kabul in November 2001, despite American and Pakistani objections, indicated partly the willingness of the Northern Alliance to demonstrate its independence. Partly, it reflected both the Iranian-Russian determination and capabilities to resist their exclusion from Afghanistan and to deny Pakistan and the United States the creation of a hostile government there. Following the Taliban's fall, Russia's dispatching of a few hundred troops to Kabul symbolically served as a reminder to the Americans and the Pakistanis of its keen interests in the future of Afghanistan. Both Iran and Russia have supported a broad-based Afghan government. However, there is no doubt that they will have little, if any, interest in such a government should their Afghan allies representing about 60 percent of the Afghans (Tajiks, Uzbeks, and Hazaris) become its junior partners. Needless to say, as an external factor, that would be a recipe for the resumption of civil war.

In general, the regional and nonregional powers involved in Afghanistan, in one form or another, are afraid of the domination on that country of a power with a potential or active hostile policy toward them. Such a scenario would create major security headaches for the regional powers. In addition to various domestic problems, including security ones, they would have to face the consequences of a hostile Afghanistan close to or along their borders. As a nonregional power, the United States would not face an immediate security threat should Afghanistan be dominated by a hostile state. However, such a scenario would deny its government a regional base to help it keep in check practically all the regional powers. Those powers have, or will likely have, conflicting interests with those of the United States in South and West Asia, two regions of importance to the Americans.

MAIN OBJECTIVES OF THE REGIONAL AMERICAN ALLIES

The Americans have found allies in the proximity of Afghanistan in what they describe as "war on terrorism." Publicly, these allies have reasoned their taking sides with the Americans on the ground of their appreciation of terrorist menace in their region and in Afghanistan. However, it is quite clear that various considerations have motivated them to join the Americans, apart from a stake in uprooting Afghanistan-based terrorist groups. In particular, it is not a secret that all of them have sought to pursue their own economic, political, and security objectives through performing their share in the war on terrorism. In this regard, certain countries have been the main protagonists, namely the Central Asian countries, China, and Pakistan. Their leaders have taken advantage of the opportunity to achieve specific objectives unrelated, if not contradictory in cases, to the objectives of their declared war on terrorism and also to that of the Americans. Apart from gaining direct and indirect economic assistance or securing American support for foreign investment and loans in return for their collaboration, the American allies have tried to achieve certain goals under the legitimate banner of fighting terrorism. The major ones are the suppression of dissent, the consolidation of authoritarianism, and an interest in changing one's international status and in weakening Russia's influence in their countries. Depending on the case, one or more than one objective may be applicable to an "ally." The following account aims at clarifying this observation.

CENTRAL ASIAN COUNTRIES

In the post–September 11 era, the emergence of a global consensus on fighting terrorism has created grounds for an opportunistic use of this broad objective by certain countries such as those in Central Asia. The latter have taken the opportunity to expand the suppression of their opposition groups under the pretext of fighting terrorism. While the iron-hand policy toward opposition groups has been a fact of life in Turkmenistan and Uzbekistan since independence, the post–September 11 era has enabled the "democratic" regimes of Kazakhstan and Kyrgyzstan to follow suit without concern about international condemnation. Despite the intention of its proponents, indiscriminate suppression of political dissent will not ensure the stability of their political systems. On the contrary, it will contribute to the radicalization of their populations only to prepare grounds for the growth of destabilizing extremist groups.

Sudden independence in 1991 imposed on the five Central Asian countries a transitional process from the Soviet command economy to a type of market economy.[32] Today, their economic systems have all the negative characteristics of the two systems while lacking most of their positive ones. Thus, they suffer from numerous problems with a direct social impact, including lowering living standards, high unemployment, and increasing poverty. Led by the Soviet elite now turned nationalist, their political systems are mainly the inherited Soviet ones without its Communist orientation, but with its shortcomings and authoritarian nature. Added to a rampant corruption, this disappointing political and economic situation has fostered a growing social discontent.

Right after independence, Tajikistan, Turkmenistan, and Uzbekistan, which were fearful of a rise of political dissent, opted for authoritarianism characterized with a policy of zero-tolerance of political dissent. In fact, both Tajikistan and Uzbekistan faced a sudden emergence of anti-government religious and nationalist groups. In the case of Tajikistan, this led to a devastating civil war that ended in 1997. In Uzbekistan's case, through an iron-hand policy, the government uprooted, severely weakened, or forced into exile all the anti-elite groups. The absence of any significant political opposition did not discourage the Turkmen elite from opting for authoritarianism, which has taken a Stalin-style form thanks to President Safarmorad Niyazov's cult of personality. Facing no significant opposition, Kazakhstan and Kyrgyzstan initially settled for relatively more tolerant political systems. Yet, the worsening economic situation and the emerging popular discontent have gradually convinced them to follow the regional trend. Today, authoritarianism has become the dominant form of government in all the Central Asian countries.[33]

Throughout Central Asia, the suppression of dissent has significantly increased in the post–September 11 era. Prior to that, concern about international condemnations made the Central Asian governments somewhat cautious in dealing with their political opponents. Their alleged crimes (e.g., posing threats to national security and damaging the prestige of leaders and governments) were hardly convincing in most cases. In the post–September 11 era, those governments have taken advantage of the situation to justify and intensify their suppression of dissent in two ways.

First, fighting Afghanistan-based terrorists has diverted the international community's attention from the abuses of human rights in many countries to the suppression of terrorists. This reality has given those governments the opportunity to continue their abuses with much less concern about international reactions, especially because their countries' geographical location has made them useful for fighting against the remnants of al-Qaeda and the Taliban in Afghanistan. Their "utility" has convinced many countries, including the United States, to turn a blind eye to their abuses. Uzbekistan and Kyrgyzstan have provided air bases for the Americans while Kazakhstan and Turkmenistan have granted overflight rights to them. Kazakhstan has also given them emergency landing rights. Regarding human rights abuses, a blatant example has been Kazakhstan. Its government suppression of opposition has intensified and taken a violent form since the 11 February 2002 speech of Kazakh President Nursultan Nazarbayev, in which he attacked opposition media for their alleged wrongdoings. Following the speech, a government crackdown on opposition has taken the form of official harassment and intimidation of the opposition media by government agents, including inspectors, auditors, and court bailiffs, who have visited all its forming members. It has also taken the form of violent attacks on publishing and printing houses as well as the intimidation of opposition journalists.

Taking place in Almaty, the following two examples should substantiate the stated claim. On 22 May 2002 "unidentified attackers" used petrol bombs to destroy the office of PR Consulting, the publisher of *Delovoye Obozrenie Respublika* (*Republic Business Review*), which is an opposition publication owned by a former cabinet minister (Mukhtar Abliazov).[34] Mr. Abliazov and Galymzhan Zhakianov, the ex-governor of Pavlodar region, have been recently arrested. They are two leaders of the Democratic Choice of Kazakhstan (DCK), a nonviolent opposition party founded in 2001 by a number of government officials and businesspeople. Reportedly, the newspaper received a warning on May 20 in the form of a decapitated dog left outside the publication's office with a note nailed to its body stating "There will be no next time."[35] The newspaper's editor-in-chief, Irina Petrushova, subsequently found the dog's head outside her house, with a similar note nailed to its skull. A few days later she received a funeral wreath. In another case on May 21, four men broke into the office of *SolDat* to beat two journalists, to steal newspaper properties, and to threaten to return if the paper continued its publication.[36] *SolDat* is an opposition newspaper connected to the Republican's People Party led by an ex-prime minister, Akezhan Kazhegeldin.

In Kyrgyzstan, the government has intensified its suppression of dissent since September 11. The "democratic" regime of President Askar Akaev began to change course in the second half of the 1990s and opted for authoritarianism. Thus, the process of consolidating this form of government began, but took a gradual form due to the absence of strong popular anti-government movements or political parties. The significant increase in popular dissent and nonviolent anti-government activities since 2000 has accelerated this process. The government has resorted to a growing high-handed policy toward dissent reflected in arrests of political dissidents, mass arrests of people involved in peaceful anti-government activities such as demonstrations, and opening fire on unarmed demonstrators. Undoubtedly, the Kyrgyz government has become more aggressive in its use of such methods since September 11. In reaction to the worsening economic situation characterized by growing unemployment and rampant corruption, the sudden increase in anti-government mass demonstrations in 2002 was met with harsh government reactions. In an incident in January the Kyrgyz government closed down several opposition newspapers and arrested Azimbek Beknazarov, a popular politician.[37] His arrest provoked popular protests especially in his home territory of Aksy district, in Jalal-Abad Province. In March, the police shot dead five demonstrators during confrontations between the police and pro-Beknazarov demonstrators.[38] This incident sparked mass demonstrations in the southern part of the country, which continued despite the dismissal by President Akaev of the prime minister and the interior minister and the resignation of the entire Kyrgyz government in May.[39] It was only when the appeal court lifted the charges against Beknazarov that the protestors went home.[40] In another incident in October 2002, clashes between police and unarmed protestors in the Province of Jalalabad left five dead and scores injured.[41]

Second, the global support for fighting against Afghanistan-based terrorists has provided a "golden" opportunity for the Central Asian governments to suppress their opposition, groups and individuals alike, under the pretext of fighting terrorists. Suddenly, they are all linked to al-Qaeda or Taliban or presented as like-minded. Hundreds of people have been arrested on unsubstantiated charges of alleged terrorist activities or links to the mentioned groups.[42] A well-known example has been the Uzbek government, which has directly connected the Islamic Movement of Uzbekistan (IMU) to those groups to justify its new wave of suppression of dissent.

The IMU is an armed fundamentalist group, but it is not a branch of al-Qaeda. As it operates in a country neighboring Afghanistan, it is quite possible that the IMU or some of its members may have had contacts with al-Qaeda and/or the Taliban protecting the latter, while using war-torn Afghanistan as a base. However, there are no similarities in the objectives and methods of al-Qaeda and the IMU to suggest their pursuit of common goals. While al-Qaeda seeks the withdrawal of the American forces from the Arab Persian Gulf countries, particularly from Saudi Arabia, and the establishment of a fundamentalist regime there, the IMU aims to replace the Uzbek government with a fundamentalist one. Its insignificant activities in other parts of the Ferghana Valley weaken the claim that it also seeks the overthrow of the Tajik and Kyrgyz governments and the creation of fundamentalist states in their countries. Al-Qaeda has committed grave atrocities against civilians, whereas the IMU has launched small-scale military operations mainly against the Uzbek security forces and to a much lesser extent against their Kyrgyz and Tajik counterparts. Prior to September 11, Uzbek President Islam Karimov's open support for establishing ties with the

Taliban in recognition of their rule over most of Afghanistan further weakens the argument on the IMU's cooperation with a group such as al-Qaeda operating in Afghanistan with the Taliban's full knowledge.

The rise of political dissent in Central Asia is a natural phenomenon caused by political, economic, and social problems. Fearful of losing power, the regional governments' banning or restricting the peaceful expression of dissent and their practical elimination of elections as the means for peaceful change of governments have created grounds for the rise of extremist ideologies. The latter promote violence as the only way to change the governments which are unable to address the mentioned problems. At the time when those governments' legitimacy is being questioned by a growing number of their respective peoples, the harsh suppression of political opponents will only increase the popularity of extremist ideologies and groups, although their envisaged political systems are even worse than the existing ones. So long as the social conditions for the rise of such groups exist, their suppression may, at best, interrupt their activities, but leave their *raison d'être* intact. Against this background, the Central Asian governments' opportunistic use of war on terrorism to legitimize their abuses of human rights will only raise doubts about fighting terrorism as a legitimate objective. It will also worsen the situation in their countries by contributing to their peoples' radicalization on which extremist groups could capitalize. Needless to say, the result will be far from the desired goal of assured stability in those countries.

Beside the suppression of dissent, the Central Asian countries have sought to weaken Russia's influence in their countries by taking sides with the American government. The collapse of the Soviet Union and the independence of the five Central Asian countries began the process of loosening ties between Russia and its former republics in Central Asia. Right after independence, Russia's cutting economic and financial assistance provided by Moscow to these countries during the Soviet period and its apparent lack of interest in extensive political and diplomatic relations with them severely weakened its relations with the Central Asian countries. However, two factors made it interested in its former Asian republics a few years after their independence. Added to its lowering international political influence, they were its economic and political failure outside the CIS while experiencing a steady economic fall at home. Hence Moscow made a move to reestablish extensive ties with the Central Asian republics in the early 1990s.[43] The Central Asians have welcomed this development to the extent necessary for their survival as they have been struggling to address their numerous transitional problems with their limited resources and meager foreign assistance. Various economic, political, social, and geographic realities make ties between the two sides an imperative, which both sides have appreciated. However, the Central Asians do not wish to restore the pre-independence pattern of relations, which will undermine their independence and put them in an inferior position vis-à-vis Russia. For that matter, they have sought to forge relations with other countries, regional and nonregional, to balance their ties with Russia, and to avoid overreliance on that country. In any case, Russia is simply unable to meet their needs in certain vital areas, first and foremost their extensive need for loans, grants, and investments.

Despite the will of the Central Asians, Russia has maintained a significant degree of influence in their region. This is partly because of the fact that various pre-independence economic, political, military, social, and linguistic links between the two sides are still in place. It is also partly because of Russia's sheer military power, which makes it a neighbor to reckon with. The Central Asians' ties with foreign countries, including Western ones, have weakened Russia's political and economic influence in its former Asian republics. However, the Western countries' lack of interest in the region, excluding in its oil-producing countries (i.e., Kazakhstan and Turkmenistan) to the extent warranted by their economic interests, has made them unreliable long-term partners for the Central Asians. This has been a major reason for their expanding ties with regional countries such as Iran and China and for their turning to Russia for economic and even military ties. For example, over ten years after their independence, Russia is still the main arms supplier to all five Central Asian countries. Also, by concluding long-term contracts in 2001 and 2002 for the use of its oil and gas pipelines, it practically controls almost the entire gas exports of Turkmenistan and about 90 percent of Kazakhstan's oil exports. For example, the June 2002 agreement between Russia and Kazakhstan provided for the transit of Kazakh oil via the Russian route of Atyrau-Samara and Makhachkala-Tikhoretsk-Novorossiisk for fifteen years.[44] The agreement stipulated that the volume of oil exported in this manner could not be less than 17.5 million tons per year.[45]

However, the American war on terrorism suddenly changed the situation. Because of their military operations in Afghanistan, the Americans turned to the Central Asian countries for air bases (Kyrgyzstan and Uzbekistan) and for overflight rights (Kazakhstan and Turkmenistan). Russia initially opposed any American military presence in the region neighboring its country, but, for a variety of reasons, it eventually lifted its opposition, which made that presence possible. The American need for the Central Asians' help significantly increased U.S. interests in their region. Such interest justifies multidimensional relations to include political, economic, and military ones. Excluding oil-related activities, the first two are still insignificant. However, if they continue and grow, those relations, and particularly, a long-term American military presence in Central Asia will sharply decrease Russia's influence in that region. Thus, the Central Asians have sought to maximize their gain out of the current American interest in their region to decrease the power and influence of Russia as a means to preserve their independence and reduce their vulnerability to Russia.

Finally, the Central Asians have seen an economic opportunity in taking sides with the United States in its war on terrorism in Afghanistan in two ways. First, the United States pays for its use of military facilities, which are so far mainly air bases. There is not any reliable publicly available report on the exact type of arrangement for their rent. However, there is no doubt that the amount paid for the use of the military facilities of Kyrgyzstan and Uzbekistan must be large enough to justify their accepting the expected hostility in regional countries such as China, Iran, and Russia. The three countries are all concerned about any significant American military presence in their proximity. Second, and more important than the latter, their taking sides with the United States will incline that country to provide various economic assistance such as loans, grants, credits, and humanitarian aid, while helping them secure favorable financial assistance such as loans in international financial markets. Having a very difficult time attracting foreign economic assistance since their independence, these Central Asian countries should really appreciate the opportunity to receive any amount of American assistance, even if it is small, in comparison to their needs, and short-term in nature. The following example reflects the difficulty that the Central Asians have experienced in securing financial assistance compared to other ex-socialist countries with much stronger ties with the Western countries. In 1999, Poland received from foreign sources $983 million in official development assistance, while Kazakhstan, Kyrgyzstan, Tajikistan, Turkmenistan, and Uzbekistan received respectively $161 million, $266.6 million, $122 million, $20.9 million, and $133.9 million.[46]

China

Like Kyrgyzstan and Uzbekistan, China has found a "reward" in taking sides with the United States in its war on terrorism. For the Chinese, this reward is not economic, but mainly political. As a matter of fact, it is not in the form of what they can extract from the Americans, but it lies in the opportunity created because of the American war in Afghanistan. The post-September era has created a basic understanding among just about all countries about the necessity of dealing with terrorism from which many countries have suffered over time in one form or another. In the absence of a widely-accepted definition of terrorism, different countries have used their self-serving definitions to justify their "counter-terrorism" activities. As well, they have built on alleged connections between their target groups with the Taliban and al-Qaeda to take advantage of the international mood mobilized against the two Afghan-based groups. For one, China has found a "golden opportunity" in the post–September 11 era to suppress the pro-independence movement in its rebellious Sinkiang Province.

As mentioned earlier, Sinkiang Province has experienced about three decades of ethnic conflict between the Uyghurs and the ethnic Chinese taking the form of an anti-government movement. The Uyghurs have resorted to a variety of political activities to achieve their main objective, independence from China. The Chinese government's resort to a zero-tolerance policy has provoked worldwide condemnation while damaging the Chinese government's international reputation. Against this background, the American war on terrorism has provided an excuse for the Chinese government to continue and to expand its harsh treatment of Uyghur anti-government groups and individuals under the more convincing pretext of "fighting terrorism." Apart from the legitimacy for fighting terrorism in the post–September 11 era, a certain act of the American government has further legitimized the suppression of the entire opposition in that province. During his visit to Beijing in August 2002, Deputy Secretary of State Richard L. Armitage announced the American State Department's adding to its list of terrorist organizations the East Turkestan Islamic Movement, a virtually unknown Uyghur organization with no significant impact on the pace of events in Sinkiang Province.[47] For the first time, the Chinese government referred to the group after the September 11 attacks on the United States by describing it as a group connected to al-Qaeda.[48] Regardless of whether the group actually has contacts with al-Qaeda, this development has made the continuation of a high-handed policy toward the entire opposition more internationally legitimate than it was before, when such a policy guaranteed only international condemnations.

Since 11 September 2001, the Chinese government has expanded its suppressive policy toward the Uyghurs, this time under the more acceptable pretext of suppressing terrorists. Internationally known human rights groups such as Amnesty International have reported extensively on this issue. In its 2002 report on the Sinkiang (Xinjiang) region of China, that organization reported grave human rights abuses since September 11 by referring to "arbitrary and summary executions, torture, arbitrary detention and unfair political trials. Particularly targeted were Uighurs [Uyghurs], . . . Thousands of political prisoners were believed to be held in [their] region."[49] The report described the situation since September 11 as follows:

A new wave of executions, of people labelled as "separatists" or "terrorists" by the authorities, took place after the 11 September attacks in the USA. A "political re-education campaign" for imams in charge of mosques in the XUAR, which was initiated in March, intensified after 11 September. Restrictions on religious practice were also placed on schools and other institutions during the holy month of Ramadan.[50]

China now claims that the Uyghur activists have been inspired, encouraged, and supplied by terrorist organizations, particularly by al-Qaeda and the Taliban stationed in neighboring Afghanistan. This is notwithstanding the fact that the Afghan territory along the Chinese border was under the Northern Alliance's control in the Taliban era, a restricting factor for any type of relationship between the Uyghurs and the Afghanistan-based terrorists.

This opportunistic use of global support for anti-terrorist campaigns will only lead to further radicalization of the Uyghurs and the expansion of instability in their province. The pro-independence movement in Sinkiang is neither homogenous nor cohesive. It consists of various large and small groups as well as many political activists subscribing to different ideologies and methods of struggle against the Chinese government. Thus, it is possible that some of them have had some sort of contact with radical or terrorist organizations in their proximity, including al-Qaeda and the Taliban. However, it is quite certain that the pro-independence movement in Sinkiang is not a creation of such organizations. Certain social realities gave birth to the movement decades before the rise of the Taliban and al-Qaeda in Afghanistan. Therefore, it cannot be branded as a terrorist creature, although foreign actors (e.g., governments, radical groups, or terrorist organizations) may have tried to use it for their own ends to a varying extent and with a differing degree of success.

The Uyghur independence movement has its roots in the social and historical realities of Sinkiang Province. The persistence of such realities, including the dissatisfaction of the Uyghurs with the status quo, has kept the movement alive despite three decades of systematic suppression. Undoubtedly, it will continue in one form or another so long as those realities remain in place. Like any other government, the Chinese government has the right to defend the territorial integrity of its country and to deal with those who resort to violent activities, including terrorists. Yet, its policy toward the Uyghur independence movement has gone far beyond those legitimate objectives to take the form of suppression of any type of dissent. Over the last three decades, that approach has failed to achieve the desired goal of ending anti-government and pro-independence sentiment and activities. There is no ground to suggest that it will have a different result in the future. Unless the Chinese government addresses the root causes of instability in Sinkiang, the continuation of its harsh policy under the pretext of "fighting terrorism" will only worsen the situation there.

Pakistan

Without any doubt, Pakistan is the main beneficiary of the American war in Afghanistan. It was the first regional country to join the American war on terrorism, which, given its role in the regional affairs, was an amazing shift in its regional policy. As the main force behind the creation of the Taliban and its last regional supporter leaving it alone only about a month prior to its fall, Pakistan's switch to the United States was a move necessitated by the sheer power of realities, not a choice made freely by the

Pakistanis. Added to the intra-conflicts in the anti-Taliban Afghan groups, the Pakistani government support of the isolated Taliban was the major foreign factor in the group's ability to stay on the political scene for about eight years and control approximately 90 percent of Afghanistan. That support made Pakistan highly isolated in the region, a very dangerous situation for a country sandwiched between its anti-Taliban traditional nuclear foe, India, and its regional rival and the main backer of the anti-Taliban Northern Alliance, Iran. Concern about the northward expansion of the Taliban made the Central Asians also suspicious about Pakistan. Its growing regional isolation matched in cases its international isolation caused by various American sanctions put in force in the 1970s and restrictions caused by its testing nuclear weapons in 1998. Added to this regional and international gloomy picture, the dismal domestic situation resulting from decades of internal feuds between and among various political groups, bloody ethnic conflicts, and a rising political extremism in various forms made the country and its government very weak.

In consequence, in the aftermath of September 11, Pakistan was in a highly vulnerable situation. As Saudi Arabia and the UAE severed ties with the Taliban a few weeks after September 11, its role as the only backer of the Taliban and the last country with diplomatic relations with it put the country in a very difficult position. Facing a global anti-Taliban mood and growing American pressure, the Pakistani government had to change its policy from seeking to save that regime to leaving it alone to face its doomed destiny. Pakistan's cutting assistance to the Taliban denied the latter the only source of economic and military support and of diplomatic connection. Such a move paved the way for the Taliban's fall in November 2001. However, Pakistan managed to get a good deal out of its last-minute maneuvering despite its well-known role in the rise and survival of the Taliban. Given the importance of its cutting ties with the Taliban as a means to facilitate the latter's fall, the Pakistani government took the opportunity to change its regional and international status and to address its numerous economic problems. All of a sudden, Pakistan, the mentor of the Taliban, changed its undesirable status from the backer of a medieval regime to a so-called frontline country at war with international terrorism fostered by the Taliban and its allies such as al-Qaeda. Its years of support of the Taliban under whose protection various terrorist organizations operated against regional and nonregional states suddenly disappeared and all the focus was given to its "sacrifices" in its taking sides with the "anti-terrorist coalition." Now, Pakistan is presented in the media as a victim of international terrorism and the key ally for the Americans in their war against the Taliban. Aside from helping Pakistan change the negative international mood toward it, the recent developments have helped the Pakistanis improve their regional standing and consolidate themselves vis-à-vis their much stronger neighboring enemy, India. Pakistan has the United States beside it now.

At least temporarily, that nonregional power sees merit in defusing conflict between the two unequal neighboring nuclear states: India and Pakistan.

The benefit of Pakistan's taking sides with the Americans is not confined to a change in its political affairs, namely its uplifted international status. At least in the short run, the Pakistanis should expect various economic rewards in the form of better treatment in international financial markets, including loans with preferential rates and repayment schedules, generous grants and aid packages, and significant investments in their country in comparison to the pre-September 11 era. These "rewards" will be provided partly by the American government and private sector and partly by other strong economies now facing no objection by the United States, which put various economic and military sanctions on Pakistan in the 1970s, the 1980s, and the 1990s. In fact, Pakistan has already received significant economic rewards from the United States, including a $500-million assistance package in late 2001.[51] In August 2002, it received a phenomenal economic gift as the American government signed a $3 billion debt forgiveness deal with its Pakistani counterpart.[52] Accordingly, Pakistan has thirty-eight years to repay the bulk of the loans—$2.3 billion—and a 15-year holiday from interest payments. Repayment of the remaining $700 million has been put on a twenty-three-year time frame, with a five-year rest from interest payments.[53] In September 2002, Pakistan received yet another financial gift, this time from the Asian Development Bank (ADB). The ADB and the Pakistani government signed a $2.4 billion agreement with the aim of reducing Pakistan's poverty from its current rate of over 30 percent to a rate below 15 percent by 2011.[54] Given this background, the Pakistanis will likely receive other large and small packages of economic assistance so long as they collaborate with the Americans in the region, provided such collaboration is necessary for their success.

Beside direct economic assistance, a major economic benefit for Pakistan of the post–Taliban era has been the possibility of turning that country into a route for international trade, particularly energy exports, of the landlocked Central Asian countries. As explained in detail before, achieving that status has been a major objective of the Pakistani government since the disintegration of the Soviet Union and the emergence of the independent states in Central Asia in 1991. Its efforts have since remained unsuccessful, despite the American preference to eliminate Iran and Russia as the major provider of transit routes to the Central Asians. For its bypassing the two countries, the Pakistani route has enjoyed the American support, but its major handicap (i.e., its reliance on Afghanistan as a connecting bridge) has made it an unreliable option, in general, and an impossible one before the fall of the Taliban. Civil war in Afghanistan and its control by various competing warlords made its use as a connecting land between Pakistan and Central Asia practically out of the question. Addressing that handicap was one of the objectives of the Pakistani government in creating the Taliban, who were hoped to end the war and to stabilize Afghanistan by eliminating all warlords. The Taliban's failure in that regard led to the shelving of the Pakistani route by major energy developers in the Caspian region. In particular, its failure led to indefinitely shelving a potentially lucrative gas pipeline between Turkmenistan and Pakistan to provide for Pakistan's domestic consumption as well as for export to other markets. In August 1998, Unocal, the project leader heading a consortium for its construction, gave up the project only to announce in the following year its decision to confine its Caspian operation to Azerbaijan.[55]

In the post–Taliban war, the end of the civil war and the hope for stability in the war-torn country has given life to the idea of the Pakistani route, in general, and the mentioned pipeline, in particular. Consequently, Pakistan, Afghanistan, and Turkmenistan signed in May 2002 an agreement for the construction of a gas pipeline to connect Turkmenistan's Daulatabad gas fields to Pakistan's port of Gwadar via Afghanistan.[56] The three countries held their first Trilateral Steering Committee to discuss the project's implementation in Ashgabat in July 2002.[57] Of course, the agreement and its follow-up meeting do not mean much in the absence of a huge foreign investment as none of the three countries has the required resources for its construction. Such an investment will be available only when Afghanistan is stable and its long-term stability is not in doubt. In the absence of such a guarantee, the implementation of the agreement seems to be highly unlikely in the foreseeable future. This is notwithstanding the ADB's reported agreement to invest in its feasibility study and to provide between 2 and 3 billion dollars for its construction provided its construction is feasible.[58]

Finally, Pakistan has sought to secure a stronger position in its dealing vis-à-vis India, its arch regional enemy, through its anti-terrorist alliance. In particular, Pakistan has failed since its 1947 independence to settle the issue of Kashmir with India, the main source of war, tension, and conflict between the two neighbors. For all practical purposes, the issue has become a forgotten case receiving no major international support for its settlement. The testing of nuclear weapons by India and Pakistan in 1998 gave some urgency to dealing with the Kashmiri dispute as it brought in the possibility of a future nuclear war over Kashmir. However, that urgency did not last long as the threat of war between the two nuclear neighbors subsided in the aftermath of the limited war of 1999 in Kargil. The conflict subsided partly as a result of American active diplomacy and partly because the two poor neighbors could not tolerate the consequences of a nuclear war or even a major conventional war. The result has been the continuation of the status quo, which serves the interest of India.

The Indians have no interest in the settlement of the Kashmir conflict as demanded by a UN resolution in the wake of their 1948 war. The resolution requires the upholding of a referendum in its controlled part of

Kashmir. The result would most probably be unfavorable for India, whether in the form of a majority vote for unification with Pakistan or in the form of a majority vote for an independent state of Kashmir. Such a negative outcome is widely expected in a predominantly Muslim region controlled by Hindu Indians since the partition of India in 1947. However, the status quo is not in the best interest of the Pakistanis who feel humiliated by the Indians as the latter defeated them on the battleground three times in 1948, 1965, and 1971. The Pakistanis thus need international backing to settle the issue by forcing India to accept serious talks over the future of Kashmir. The sudden importance of Pakistan for the Americans in the pursuit of their regional interests has provided Pakistan with the backing of the United States regarding a settlement for the status of Kashmir. Yet, it is not certain how long the American interests in Pakistan will remain in place and to what extent the Americans are inclined to use their influence to settle the issue.

Beside an interest in helping an ally for as long as its collaboration is necessary, concern about a war between India and Pakistan has created an additional incentive for the American government to help the two sides settle the Kashmir dispute. Such a war would inevitably shift the current focus on terrorism to a war with a potential of escalating into a nuclear one. In 2002, various bloody attacks on Indian targets in the Indian-controlled Kashmir and in Delhi by Kashmiri militants operating from their bases in Pakistan provoked the concentration of the Indian troops along the cease-fire line in Kashmir. Unsurprisingly, Pakistan matched that military move as the two sides prepared themselves for a possible war. The Americans have sought to calm both sides and to put pressure on Pakistan to rein in the Kashmiri militants as a necessary move to avoid a war between the two neighbors.

Although it is not clear how far the Americans are prepared to go to end the Kashmiri dispute, there is no question that the issue of Kashmir has been put on the international agenda in the post–September 11 era. At the minimum, even a limited interest of the Americans could help Pakistan decrease the possibility of a war with India. Regardless of its conventional or nuclear nature, the Pakistanis cannot possibly hope to win a war with India because of their significant weaknesses in both fields.[59] In short, Pakistan seems to be the major regional beneficiary of the American war on terrorism in South and West Asia.

Saudi Arabia

As the largest and most populous Southern Persian Gulf country, Saudi Arabia is the most important American ally in the Persian Gulf. Like many other regional countries, it also joined the loose American camp against terrorism in 2001. For the Saudis, fighting al-Qaeda and like-minded groups is very much within their national interests. That group has been a major threat to the stability of the Saudi regime because of its involvement in bloody acts of terror in Saudi Arabia and also for its declared objective of toppling the Saudi regime. Al-Qaeda has demonized that regime for its close ties with the American government and particularly for its granting military bases to the Americans who have kept significant numbers of troops there since 1990. Being a rich oil-exporting country of interest to many Western and non-Western countries, Saudi Arabia has no strong economic incentive for its cooperation with the Americans. Nor has it been offered any specific economic incentive. As a result, the main objective of the Saudis in joining the American camp has been security considerations. This is of course in addition to the expected cooperation of a country like Saudi Arabia, which has long been the largest American ally in the strategically important Persian Gulf region.

However, Saudi Arabia has been the most reluctant American ally in its war on terrorism. By no means does it imply any complicity of the Saudi government in terrorist activities in general and those of al-Qaeda in particular. On the contrary, as stated by different American officials, it has cooperated with the American government in its fight against al-Qaeda. This is quite logical as the group founded and run mainly by Saudis and/or those of Arab countries in its proximity is a much stronger long-term threat to that country's security than it is to the United States. Nevertheless, a variety of factors have discouraged the Saudis to become an enthusiastic ally of the United States in its war on terrorism, of which two factors have been especially important.

One factor is the ambiguity about the real objective that the American government seeks to achieve in its war on terrorism. In the wake of the September 11 terrorist attacks, the American efforts to punish those responsible were both justified and understandable for everyone inside and outside the Persian Gulf, like elsewhere. Thus, the overthrow of the Taliban and the military efforts to uproot the remnants of the group and those of al-Qaeda received the backing of almost all the regional and nonregional countries. Parallel to that, the destruction of the group's cell all over the world was also accepted by all states. However, the war on terrorism has since expanded to include other objectives such as "regime change" in Iraq and also to expand to a variety of countries of no clear relevance to uprooting al-Qaeda, including Georgia where the Americans maintain military advisers. Such developments have raised questions about the long-term objectives of the United States and whether the initially legitimate objective has now been used to justify the American military presence in certain important regions for the American government, namely the Persian Gulf, the Caucasus, and Central Asia.

Another factor has been the American policy toward the Middle East. Seen as one-sided and clearly pro-Israeli in the Middle East, that policy has contributed to a growing anti-American sentiment all over the Arab countries. It has been reflected in an increasing number of anti-American demonstrations in even pro-American countries such as Jordan, Egypt, and Morocco. Such sentiment has put Arab countries, all of which suffer from domestic political dissent and unpopularity, if not outright illegitimacy, in a very weak position. Taking sides with the Americans at the time when Israel's high-handed policy toward the Palestinians has outraged not only the Arabs, but also the Europeans, has become a very dangerous political stance. Saudi Arabia is not an exception to this situation. As an example, the boycott of American soft drinks in that country and other Arab countries such as Bahrain, the base of the American Fifth Fleet in the Persian Gulf, and a sudden growth in demand for Iranian soft drinks (Zamzam Cola and Iran Cola) reflect that reality.[60] At least for the mentioned reasons, the Saudis have sought to limit their support of the American war on terrorism to their joint activities against al-Qaeda, a source of threat to the two countries to a varying extent.

NOTES

1. The Global Development Briefing (GDB hereafter), 12 September 2002. (Internet publication)

2. Ibid.

3. GDB, 10 October 2002.

4. Ibid.

5. Ibid.

6. Kate Clark, "Simmering Feuds," *Middle East International*, 16 August 2002, 22.

7. Ibid.

8. Ibid.

9. Hooman Peimani, "Afghanistan-Based International Drug-Trafficking: A Continued Threat," *Central Asia-Caucasus Analyst* (Baltimore), 8 May 2002.

10. Clark, 22.

11. Ibid.

12. GDB, 26 September 2002.

13. Kevin Miller, Jr., kevmille@indiana.edu, "Afghanistan: UN Optimistic after Government Moves on Opium," Central Asia News, 5 April 2002 22:23:48 -0500. (Internet publication)

14. Ibid.

15. News, Radio of the Islamic Republic of Iran, 14 October 2002.

16. "The World This Week," *The Economist*, 31 August 2002, 6.

17. GDB, 26 September 2002.

18. Ibid.

19. News, 14 October 2002.

20. Miller, Jr.

21. The World This Week, 6.

22. Ibid.

23. GDB, 17 October 2002.

24. Ibid.

25. "Guard Tries to Kill President," *Guardian* (unlimited), 5 September 2002.

26. "Iranian President Condemns Assassination Attempt on President Karzai," *Ettela'at Binolmelali* (Tehran), 9 August 2002, 2.

27. Thom Shanker with John F. Burns, "State Department to Take Over Security for Afghan Leader," *The New York Times,* 25 August 2002. (Internet version)

28. Aftab Kazi and Tariq Saeedi, "India and the Politics of the Trans-Afghan Gas Pipeline," *Central Asia—Caucasus Analyst* (Baltimore), 28 August 2002. (Internet version)

29. Clark, 23.

30. Ibid., 22.

31. Ibid.

32. For a detailed account on the state of the political and economic situation in the Central Asian countries right after independence and in the 1990s, see: Hooman Peimani, *Regional Security and the Future of Central Asia: The Competition of Iran, Turkey, and Russia* (Westport, CT: Praeger, 1998), 27–30, 92–95; Hooman Peimani, *Iran and the United States: The Rise of the West Asian Regional Grouping* (Westport, CT: Praeger, 1999), 7–10.

33. For a detailed discussion about the domination of authoritarianism in Central Asia and the Caucasus, including its success in securing the desired objectives, see: Hooman Peimani: *Failed Transition, Bleak Future? War and Instability in Central Asia and the Caucasus* (Westport, CT: Praeger, 2002).

34. Joldas Babaev, "Kazak Journalists Face Brutal Intimidation: Unidentified Hooligans Wage Reign of Terror on Opposition Journalists," From: "kevmille," kevmille@indiana.edu, Central Asia News, 30 May 2002 06:58:36 -0000. (Internet publication)

35. Ibid.

36. Ibid.

37. "Kyryzstan Political Crisis," International Crisis Group Media Release (Osh/Brussels), 20 August 2002.

38. Ibid.

39. Ibid.

40. Ibid.

41. GDB, 10 October 2002.

42. See: Amnesty International reports for 2001 and 2002.

43. For details on the circumstances under which Russia and the Central Asian countries became interested in expanding ties, see: Peimani, *Regional Security and the Future of Central Asia,* pp. 27–36, 54–55, 69–75, 92–95.

44. "Kazakhstan and Russia Sign Agreement on Oil Transit," volume 7, issue #13—Thursday, June 27, 2002. (Internet version)

45. Ibid.

46. UNDP, *Human Development Report 2001* (New York: Oxford University Press, 2001), 191–192.

47. Eril Eckholm, "American Gives Beijing Good News: Rebels on Terror List," *The New York Times,* 26 August 2002. (Internet version)

48. Ibid.

49. "China: Xinjiang Uighur Autonomous Region," *Amnesty International Report 2002.* (Internet version)

50. Ibid.

51. "Pakistan Stuns Airbus, Opt for Boeing," *Asia Times online* (Hong Kong), 28 August 2002.

52. Ibid.

53. Ibid.

54. GDP, 19 September 2002.

55. "Iran's New Agreements on Energy," *Eurasian File* (Ankara), 112 (January 1999): 7.

56. Kazi and Saeedi.

57. Ibid.

58. Ibid.

59. For an assessment of the Indian and Pakistani conventional military capabilities, the strength of their nuclear arsenals, and the availability of means of delivery of nuclear weapons, including aircraft, missiles, and submarines, see: Hooman Peimani, *Nuclear Proliferation in the Indian Subcontinent: The Self-Exhausting "Superpowers" and Emerging Alliances* (Westport, CT: Praeger, 2000), 17–21, 53, 76–79.

60. REF/RL, August.

4

Creation of the Two Rival Camps

The "anti-terrorist" cooperation between the United States and a number of countries in South and West Asia cannot last very long. In the post–September 11 era, the American declared "war on terrorism" created grounds for the creation of an anti-terrorist "alliance" in South and West Asia. The regional partners of the United States in its war, namely China, Russia, India, Pakistan, and certain Persian Gulf and Central Asian countries, found opportunities in their loose alliance, which were implicit in most cases. The alliance was vague enough in terms of objectives and broad enough in terms of means to accommodate the national and/or regional objectives of all of them. The common denominator was the necessity of toppling the Taliban for its posing security threats to all the regional countries, excluding Pakistan, and for its harboring terrorist organizations, including al-Qaeda. Beyond that, the declared objective of "fighting terrorism" was not a uniting factor for the alliance members with different sets of concerns and priorities in mind. This was due to the absence of any serious effort on the part of the alliance members to define clearly what constitutes terrorism and where, how, and by whom it should be fought and for what objectives. Lacking common, clear long-term objectives, the alliance also lacked a clear plan of action to achieve certain well-defined objectives, a timetable to meet them, and a clear organizational form. Unsurprisingly, the loose alliance was bound to fall apart gradually after a short while of cooperation.

From the very beginning, the implicit alliance had elements of disunity requiring only a certain situation to make the alliance partners go their separate ways. What kept the alliance together in the beginning was the clear objective of fighting Afghanistan-based terrorist groups, mainly the Taliban and al-Qaeda. Apart from Pakistan, all other alliance members suffered to a varying degree from the Taliban rule in Afghanistan and its patronage of terrorist organizations. Thus, the so-called partners had their incentives to support the campaign to uproot the Taliban and all its protégés, including al-Qaeda. However, the Taliban's fall changed the situation dramatically, although its fall did not lead to the total destruction of the group and al-Qaeda. Surely, all the regional countries, including Pakistan, are still concerned about the regrouping of the two groups and their acts of revenge against all the regional countries, including Pakistan, for their backing the Americans. Nevertheless, while fighting the remnants of those groups has remained an issue for all of them, it can no longer be an objective strong enough to keep them together. About two years after the Taliban's fall, fighting the remnants of the two groups for their role in the September 11 terrorist attacks remains a priority only for the Americans.

The Taliban's fall created a new regional environment, which led the countries involved in its downfall to think about the political and security makeup of their regions in the post–Taliban era. In fact, certain developments have contributed to a gradual emergence of conflicting long-term interests within the rank of anti-terrorist "allies" and in their regions with an inevitable negative impact on the pattern of cooperation in late 2001. Thus, in a suitable environment created over time, this reality has created grounds for the polarization of the two neighboring regions, South and West Asia, connected to each other via Afghanistan. As will be discussed, certain factors have set the polarization process in motion.

IMPACT OF THE UNITED STATES ON THE POLARIZATION PROCESS

South and West Asia have gone through a process of polarization. Without a doubt, this process began in a suitable environment for whose creation many factors have helped over time. However, a sudden change in the security makeup of those regions in late 2001 functioned as a catalyst in the polarization process, while ensuring its direction to a great extent. The deployment of the American military forces in Afghanistan and Central Asia brought about this change and began a new era in the political structure of South and West Asia. The latter was not only a result of the fall of the Taliban regime, a menace for almost all its neighbors, but also the consequence of the unintentional impact of that development on the political and security structure of the two regions. The sudden change in their balance of power resulting from the deployment of American military forces and the taking sides of certain regional countries with the United States changed the security makeup of those regions completely. The resulting sudden increase in the American political and military presence acted as a stimulus to change drastically the overall regional situation, including the security makeup of those regions. This stimulus initiated a process of political polarization leading to the gradual creation of two camps or groupings with opposite long-term objectives. The competition and confrontation of these two camps will likely have long-term consequences for South and West Asia as well as other regions connected to them in one way or another.

The increase in the American political and military presence in South and West Asia has activated the process of polarization by provoking regional reactions. In particular, such reactions have demonstrated themselves in the forms of two major concerns. One is a growing concern about the long-term regional objectives of the United States. Another is a concern about instability in Afghanistan and its impact on its respective region in different forms.

GROWING AMERICAN INFLUENCE IN CENTRAL ASIA, THE CAUCASUS, AFGHANISTAN, AND PAKISTAN

Undoubtedly, concern about the long-term objectives of the United States in the region has been the single major factor in the process of polarization. Prior to the September 11 terrorist attacks, the American influence in Central Asia and the Caucasus was mainly confined to economic and political spheres. The domination of the American oil companies on the vast energy resources of the Caspian region was, of course, a source of anxiety for the regional powers because of its negative economic implications for them. As well, they were concerned about its corresponding political influence for the Americans with an inevitable weakening impact on the regional powers. However, in the post–September 11 era, the Americans have added a strong military dimension to their political and economic presence in those regions, making their overall presence a serious menace to, or at least a serious source of concern for the regional powers. The American government's war on terrorism in Afghanistan has enabled it to deploy military forces in Central Asia, the Caucasus, Afghanistan, and Pakistan, while suddenly expanding its military presence in the Persian Gulf. Added to their permanent significant military bases in Turkey, the extensive American military presence in South and West Asia has created anxiety for China, Iran, India, and Russia.

If the current trend continues, the countries hosting American military forces will gradually become permanent U.S. military bases from where the United States could project its power in the regions close to those countries. The American military presence in Afghanistan and in certain countries in its proximity, that is Kyrgyzstan and Uzbekistan, has been a realistic source of concern for China, Iran, and Russia since the arrival of the first American units in October 2001. Sharing long borders with Afghanistan and/or Central Asia, they were suspicious of the long-term objectives of the Americans in their region where they have strategic interests. As mentioned earlier, that region is also of interest to the Americans for its significant oil and gas resources and for the potential role it could play in "containing" the three regional powers that have reasons for grievances with the United States.

In the aftermath of September 11, Russia's opposition to the stationing of American military forces close to its borders in Central Asia and the Caucasus caused its neighboring Central Asian states to reject the idea of letting American forces use their territories for their operation in Afghanistan. However, certain factors convinced the Russians to change their position and to get credit for their cooperative policy in their future dealings with the Americans. They included Russia's interest in the Taliban regime's fall, its interest in expanding economic ties with the United States requiring friendly bilateral relations, and its concern about a possible acceptance of American request for bases by Central Asians despite its opposition. To allay the Russian concern, many American military and civilian officials stressed in late 2001 the short-term nature of the American military presence in Central Asia and Afghanistan and the immediate withdrawal of their troops once their military operation was over. However, Russia, along with Iran and China, was well aware that the Americans might use the opportunity to stay in the region long after meeting their announced military objectives.

The well-known American political and economic interests in Central Asia and the Caucasus aside, the pattern of American military deployment in Central Asia and the Persian Gulf unjustifiable for a limited warfare in Afghanistan served as a clear indicator of such a probability. Having secured an air base in Uzbekistan neighboring Afghanistan, the Americans also obtained the right to use another air base, this time in Kyrgyzstan without any apparent necessity or usefulness, as the country does not share a border with Afghanistan. The Kazakh government turned down a U.S. request for a third air base in Kazakhstan, a country far from Afghanistan. However, it granted them overflight and emergency landing rights, while the Americans received overflight rights from Turkmenistan as well. Despite their buildup in Central Asia and Afghanistan, the Americans also heavily deployed their naval and air forces in the Persian Gulf and the Arabian Sea with no obvious direct relevance to their type of operation in landlocked Afghanistan separated from the Arabian Sea by Pakistan. While maintaining their bases in Saudi Arabia, they secured new bases in Oman and Qatar, expanded their forces in Kuwait and Bahrain, and received overflight rights from the UAE. Given the extent of the American military deployment in Central Asia and the Persian Gulf, the whole declared "anti-terrorist" military preparation seemed, and still seems, totally unproportional to the declared objective of uprooting the remnants of the Taliban and al-Qaeda armed mainly with light weapons.

About two years after the first American units entered the region, the American military presence now seems to last long after the end of the war in Afghanistan, a suspicion confirmed by clear statements of high-ranking American officials. In his 23 August 2002 meeting with Uzbek President Islam Karimov in Tashkent, General Tommy L. Franks, commander of the American forces in Afghanistan, Central Asia, and the Persian Gulf, announced what many states, including Russia, Iran, and China, had long been concerned about. Meeting President Karimov after visiting Kyrgyzstan and Kazakhstan, he stated that the American military presence in Central Asia and Afghanistan would increase, the Americans would expand their military relations with the Central Asian countries, and the American forces would stay longer than expected in Afghanistan.[1] On the same day, an American Congressional delegation visiting Tashkent stressed the American government's determination to stay in the region.[2]

A long-term American military presence in South and West Asia will be a direct security threat to Iran, India, China, and Russia. It will also be a threat to their regional interests, including a predictably significant loss in their power, influence, and economic interests. If the Americans can turn the Afghan central government into a fully functional pro-American government, a pro-American Afghanistan will be a major threat for all the regional powers that either share borders with or are in close proximity to Afghanistan. Hence, these powers are understandably worried about the direction of developments in Afghanistan. Added to the growing American influence and military presence elsewhere in the regions in its proximity, a pro-American Afghan government will put the United States in a very strong position to influence the pace of events in South and West Asia.

The mentioned statements of American military and political figures, including those of General Franks, contradicted the American government's previous assurances for its forces' short stay in the region, but they should not surprise the Chinese, the Iranians, and the Russians. Nevertheless, the resulting expansion of the American forces in Central Asia and Afghanistan will surely contribute to the worsening American ties with Iran, China, and Russia. The American decision for long-term stay in West Asia signifies an emerging hostile American foreign policy toward the three mentioned countries whose elements have been surfacing since the election of President George W. Bush. Added to its deploying military "advisers" in Georgia in early 2002 and to its growing military ties with Azerbaijan, the long-term American military presence in Central Asia will create serious security concerns for Iran, China, and Russia, making them more inclined to group together in face of the American threat. Russia's fear about its encirclement by hostile countries will strengthen its ties with the other two countries and in particular with Iran, a large neighboring country that shares that fear. The two countries' multidimensional bilateral relations have been on a friendly path since the last years of the Soviet Union.

While its friendly ties with Iran and China are not a new development, Russia's efforts to restore its extensive Soviet-era relations with Iraq and North Korea have reflected symbolically the consolidation of a new turn in Russian foreign policy. They indicate not only its efforts to regain its lost markets, but also its clear attempt to pursue its national interests without regard to American disapproval. Russia now seeks to demonstrate its fundamental differences with the United States over various international issues, including ties with certain countries on uneasy terms with the United States. That is part of its bid to reestablish its lost preeminent international status by capitalizing on a new Russian foreign policy not aligned with that of the United States. Having that objective in mind, the Russian government announced plans for major contracts with Iran and Iraq in early August 2002. Thus, it disclosed preparing an agreement with Iran to sell $5 billion worth of advanced weapons and to expand their annual trade to $5 billion, while expressing readiness to sell six more nuclear power reactors to Iran.[3] It also announced a plan for a $40 billion economic pact with Iraq mainly related to the Iraqi oil industry. Finally, in the same month, President Vladimir Putin met with North Korean President Kim Il-Jong in Vladivostock. During the meeting, in tune with his plan to turn Russia into the major route for Asian-European trade, he stressed his country's interest in connecting South Korean railways to the Russian rail network via North Korea and China.[4] Iran's troubled relations with the United States are not something new, but Russia's seeking closer ties with the members of the "axis of evil" in August 2002 symbolically demonstrated the practical end of its "honeymoon" with the United States. Also, it indicated the beginning of an era of tension and conflict in American-Russian relations.

Concern about the Stability of Afghanistan

Concern about the pace of events inside Afghanistan has been another major contributing factor to the process of polarization. After the initial happiness in the region about the Taliban's fall, the issue of stability became a worrisome issue for all those with stakes in that country. Theoretically, the civil war was over, but the resumption of war could well be a matter of time as its core causes were yet to be tackled. In particular, the absence of a widely-acceptable and fully-functional central government was the main source of concern, which has continued to this date. So long as this situation persists, the resumption of civil war remains a very realistic scenario, as reflected in fighting between warlords in different parts of the country. This fragile situation indicates that regional, ethnic, and religious conflicts suppressed to a great extent under the Taliban regime have reemerged. As well, it demonstrates that the political, tribal, and religious leaders representing the diversified Afghan ethnic and religious groups have failed to come to a power-sharing agreement in tune with the realities of the country and thus acceptable to all the concerned groups. Lack of such consensus is a recipe for another round of civil war. Consequently, the persistence of instability in Afghanistan has been a major source of concern. The latter paves the way for the rise or re-rise of all vices stemming from an unstable situation, as has been the case for the last two decades.

As sad as it may sound, the process of government-building in Afghanistan has been a failure. This is notwithstanding the efforts of the central government led by Mr. Hamid Karzai, a government proven to be too weak to address the major problems. The latter does not have any power outside Kabul where it is even unable to ensure the security of its senior officials. As mentioned earlier, in 2002, two senior figures, Afghan Minister for Air Transport and Tourism Abdul Rahman and a vice-president, Haji Abdul Qadir, were killed in Kabul,[5] while President Karzai became a target of an unsuccessful assassination attempt.[6] Bombing has become a common occurrence in many Afghan cities, including Kabul. A recent blatant example was a powerful blast in September 2002 in that city, which left about 180 people killed and wounded.[7] In another incident in September, a car bomb in Kabul at a city market near the ministries of information and education killed at least fifteen people, and possibly many more.[8] Bombing and attacks on government forces and employees all over Afghanistan increased in 2003.

Outside Kabul, the country is practically run by warlords. The Kabul government has been unable to expand its influence beyond Kabul or at least establish a degree of stability in the country. In particular, the existing fragile and chaotic situation has become especially alarming for those countries neighboring Afghanistan, mainly Iran, China, and the Central Asian countries, whose worries are also shared by Russia. They are all concerned about the direct and indirect impact of instability in Afghanistan on their countries, for example, the "export" of instability to their countries, the radicalization of their dissatisfied peoples, and the inflow of small arms and refugees into their countries. As well, they are concerned about the turning of Afghanistan into a safe haven for their extremist anti-government organizations, as was the case under the Taliban regime.

To have a complete picture of the situation, one should also add the fear of extensive Afghanistan-based international drug-trafficking. There has been a surge in opium production in Afghanistan in the post–Taliban era. Various sources estimated the 2002 crop to be between 3,000 and 4,000 tons, very close to the peak production of 4,600 tons in 1999.[9] The 2003 crop should be in that range if not larger. Iran has been the major regional victim of such trafficking resulting in the loss of over 3,350 law enforcement personnel over the last two decades, and in the existence of over 2 million drug addicts. To this picture, one should add the negative impact on the Iranian society of associated crimes such as small arms trafficking and armed robbery. With a growing number of addicts, the Central Asians and Russia have also been victims because their countries have become the scene of drug-related crimes. In particular, this phenomenon has become a serious problem for Russia facing a bloody armed conflict in Chechnya, while its drug addicts are estimated to be between 3 and 4 million according to a 2001 estimate.[10] Given the weaknesses of the Afghan central government and the expansion of warlords all over the country, the expansion of the Afghan drug "industry" seems to be a sure bet, unless the prevailing situation changes somehow. The latter is an unrealistic scenario in the foreseeable future.

REGIONAL FACTORS CONTRIBUTING TO THE POLARIZATION PROCESS

South and West Asia have contained the seeds of polarization for quite some time. Unlike many other regions of the world, there is a heavy concentration of regional powers that are dissatisfied with their current regional and international status. Iran, India, China, Russia, and Pakistan have large conventional military forces, while the last four states also have nuclear capabilities of a varying magnitude. All of them have major long-term interests in South and West Asia arising from their economic interests, political objectives, and security considerations. As regional powers, any major development in those regions will have serious positive or negative consequences for them, which could weaken or strengthen their positions. As a nonregional power, the United States is a fully fledged superpower with strong long-term interests in those regions. All these regional and nonregional powers have reasons for rivalry stemming from their pursuit of long-term interests. Over time, certain factors will lead to their groupings, although they may remain fluid, leaving room for defections from one group to another. Thus, South and West Asia are heading toward polarization. If the current situation continues, this ongoing process will eventually lead to the creation of two rival camps consisting of Iran, India, and Russia with which China will be affiliated at least for awhile, and of the United States and Pakistan. Many small regional countries will take sides with one or another based on their perception of threat and needs at any given period of time. They will function as short-term allies or friends with questionable commitment to their camp members.

For a variety of reasons, Pakistan was the only firm and declared regional ally of the United States when the anti-terrorist alliance was created in late 2001. As mentioned earlier, various factors pushed the Pakistanis to side with the Americans. In particular, political, security, and, of course, economic incentives inclined them to sacrifice their Afghan protégé. Cutting the support line to Taliban via Pakistan and suppressing the pro-Taliban and/or al-Qaeda extremist groups at home seemed important measures for the elimination of Afghanistan-based terrorist groups as well as fighting them in Afghanistan. Hence, the United States and Pakistan emerged as natural allies, creating the so-called frontline states at war with Afghanistan-based terrorist organizations, even though Pakistan was not directly involved in military operations in Afghanistan. Convergence of interests helped the creation of an explicit alliance between the two countries that need each other to pursue their short- and long-term objectives.

However, other regional countries (Iran, India, China, Russia, and the Central Asian and the Persian Gulf countries) accepted the legitimacy of the declared objectives in Afghanistan. They also contributed to its success to the extent justified by their national interests and particularly by their perception of threat rising from Afghanistan. Consequently, from the beginning, there was a natural division within the alliance based on the objectives of the involving countries and their degree of closeness to the United States. This natural division soon became deeper as other interrelated factors came into effect. The result has been the emergence of a suitable ground for the rise of two rival camps of states in South and West Asia.

As is the case in any other phenomenon, there are many parameters responsible for the creation of these two rival camps. They include historical factors and geographical realities, common concerns and problems, and shared interests. They also include short- and long-term needs and political and security considerations functioning as both incentives and imperatives for close ties between and among certain countries. The latter have created natural grounds for close ties and collaboration among two groups of states.

Factors for Iran, India, Russia, and China

For a variety of reasons, there is a natural tendency toward cooperation and friendship among and between Iran, India, and Russia. Despite their different historical, political, economic, and military backgrounds, they are dissatisfied regional powers for all practical purposes. This is notwithstanding Russia's former status as a fully-fledged superpower and its current formidable nuclear capability. Technically, that capability makes it a military superpower, although severe economic problems make the Russians unable to preserve this military superiority. This was reality, the main reason behind their 2002 agreement with the Americans to reduce the size of their nuclear arsenal. For all its weaknesses, Russia has been demoted to the status of a regional power since the Soviet Union's fall. It has since sought to create a sphere of influence to address many of its political, economic, and military/security problems. Against this background, Russia has at least four issues in common with Iran and India, which compel them to collaborate with each other.

Common Sense of Dissatisfaction

Iran, India, and Russia share a common sense of dissatisfaction with the existing international system for different reasons. For Russia, the loss of its preeminent status only matched by its arch rival, the United States, has been the major source of dissatisfaction. The fall of the Soviet Union not only ended the Cold War bipolar international system, it also ended Russia's role as a major actor in world affairs. That country has lost all its former bloc members of whom most have switched to the United States, while being unable to establish a new bloc. This is a result of its loss of political influence and economic strength and its eroding military might. Facing numerous political, economic, and social problems at home, it has transferred all its limited resources to addressing its own problems leaving practically nothing to be spared for building a new "empire." Russia's preoccupation with its internal affairs and its dismal economic situation have made it dependent on Western financial sources for its development programs. This reality has removed Russia from the international political scene as an influential actor. Undoubtedly, it is incapable of affecting the pace of events in major international events. Despite its status as a permanent member of the United Nations Security Council (UNSC), it has become a completely marginalized nuclear state without a power corresponding to that formidable might. In short, Russia has descended from the superpower status leading a bloc of states in different continents to the status of a regional power without any sphere of influence, while suffering from various domestic problems.

India has been dissatisfied with the international system ever since it gained independence in 1947. For its severe long-term impact on their society, its independence itself became a source of grievance with that system. The Indians achieved independence as part of an agonizing process of partition of their territory into two hostile separate states of India and Pakistan. Among other problems, the unsettled dispute over the status of Jammu and Kashmir set grounds for decades of conflict and hostility between the two neighbors, which has lasted to this date. Coming out of centuries of colonization, India emerged as an independent country with a wide range of difficulties and underdevelopment for which there was no immediate remedy. As a huge country with a very large and growing population and with an ancient civilization, the Indians expected an eminent role in international affairs unattainable with their weak economy and insignificant military power.

The initiation of the Cold War around the time of their independence forced them to side with one of the two leading polls. For the Indians, the choice was the one reflecting their anger with their former colonizers, while offering the badly needed help especially in the form of technology transfer. The Indians did not join the Soviet bloc as an official member, but, thanks to their extensive ties with that bloc and especially with the Soviet Union itself, they enjoyed most of its benefits without losing their independence. India's well-established ties with the Soviet Union laid the foundation of its current friendly and extensive political, economic, and military ties with Russia. The Indians' allegiance with the Soviet bloc helped them expand their scientific, technological, and military capabilities, but it did not improve drastically their international status. Beside its military signifi-cance, India's efforts to emerge as a nuclear power have reflected its aspi-ration to upgrade its international status. Hence it wishes to be accepted not just as a large regional power, but as a global power, and eventually as a superpower to be reckoned with in all world affairs.[11] India also views a nuclear capability as a ticket to its future permanent membership in the UNSC.

However, despite its official entry in the nuclear club in 1988, India is far from being considered and treated as a superpower or even a global power equal to other UNSC members or major economies such as Japan and Germany. As a result, India has remained a dissatisfied regional power whose bid to attain an eminent international status has been prevented by the existing international system discriminating against aspiring newcomers. Unsurprisingly, in the post–Cold War era, the Indians have become propo-nents of a multipolar system in which India could achieve eminent status as a poll. India has therefore remained opposed to the creation of an American-led unipolar international system, which, if created, will ensure the prolongation of India's current dissatisfactory status. Despite this atti-tude, India has cozied up to the United States to gain access to its large and lucrative market, a target of the Indian software industry, to attract its investments, and to receive its advanced technology.

Iran is also a dissatisfied regional power. Its 1979 revolution, despite its religious rhetoric, was an eruption of Iranian nationalism seeking to remove the barriers to its reemergence as a strong regional power, if not a global one, influential in Asia, Eurasia, and the Middle East. These are three regions to which it has geographical, historical, and social links. For the last time, Iran lost its global status in 1828, when after two series of devastat-ing wars with the emerging Russian empire it finally accepted the secession of the Caucasus and Russia's sovereignty over it as it signed the Turkmanchai Treaty.[12] Although the process of Iran's demise began a few decades earlier, the treaty symbolically marked its loss of an eminent status and began a process of decline that lasted for about one and a half cen-turies, despite its economic and military progress in the twentieth century. After about four decades of membership in the American bloc, the 1979 revolution enabled Iran to seek an identity on its own merits as an aspiring regional power. That development brought for Iran real political indepen-dence in place of the nominal one under the Shah regime, undermined by the strong American political, economic, and military presence in Iran. Yet, the new reality has not paved Iran's way to an eminent status for which it has all the ingredients. They include a large area with different climatic regions, a large and growing population, richness in minerals and fossil energy resources, access to open seas, strategic location with military, political, and economic values, a large class of educated professionals, an extensive infrastructure, a significant industrial basis, and a large agriculture sector.

On the contrary, a variety of factors has prevented it from reaching that status, while making it politically isolated and economically exhausted.

The hoped-for process of economic, scientific, and military advancement to back Iran's claim to a higher international status has not materialized. Undoubtedly, many internal factors have been responsible for this failure, including the religious and extremist nature of the Iranian regime, the incompetence of the ruling elite, political disputes between rival ruling factions, extensive mismanagement of the country, and rampant corruption. However, there have also been major external factors contributing to that failure. They include various European and American economic sanctions on Iran, politically- and economically-motivated barriers to its international trade, its politically-motivated exclusion from major international organizations (e.g., WTO) and lucrative regional economic projects (e.g., Caspian energy projects), and the devastating Iran-Iraq war (1980–1988). Apart from its heavy casualty of about 1.5 million dead and wounded, that war inflicted astronomical damage on Iran's industries, agriculture, infrastructure, environment, and private properties estimated at about one trillion dollars.

In spite of the external and internal barriers, Iran has made significant advancement in addressing its industrial, agricultural, educational, and military shortcomings since 1979.[13] Yet, it still suffers from numerous economic problems, technological stagnation or underdevelopment in areas such as high tech, and from dependency on foreign suppliers for advanced military and non-military industrial goods. Briefly, many external and internal factors have created an obstacle to Iran's creation of corresponding economic, scientific, and military institutions to consolidate its political independence. This failure has denied the Iranians their desired status of a strong regional power with interests in certain regions in its proximity (i.e., the Persian Gulf, the Middle East, the Indian Ocean, Central Asia, and the Caucasus).

For all practical purposes, and despite its various shortcomings, Iran has become a regional power with a degree of influence in the mentioned regions. However, this is far less limited than the Iranians have hoped to achieve, because there are many external factors in place to limit their progress in all areas of domestic and foreign fields. Therefore, Iran sees itself as a victim of the international system. This system has prevented its rise as an influential power through a variety of means, including the Iraqi invasion of Iran in 1980, which turned into a long war of attrition. The Iraq-instigated war was encouraged, assisted, or tolerated by a variety of regional and nonregional powers, including major Western powers. Moreover, Iran has also been barred from making its influence felt in many regional issues of direct impact on it or of importance to its security. The security arrangement in the Persian Gulf, the division of the Caspian Sea among its littoral states, the development and the export of the Caspian oil and natural gas resources, and the Arab-Israeli conflict are just to name a few. In reality, Iran has been marginalized in world politics.

China also has reasons for dissatisfaction with the international system. The years of domination and occupation by and war with Western powers and Japan in the nineteenth and the twentieth centuries have created grounds for its deep mistrust and resentment of foreign powers whose hostile acts toward it have been permitted and justified by the international system. As a replacement of the hostile multipolar system, the bipolar systems of the post–World War II era gradually became even more dangerous to the Chinese as both leading powers, the Soviet Union and the United States, became hostile to them. The last decade of the Cold War became less dangerous, thanks to China's rapprochement with the United States and the effort on the part of the Soviet leaders to ease tension with their Chinese neighbors during the last years of their rule. The end of the bipolarity created hope for a better treatment for China in the rising multipolarity in which China is a pole. However, the efforts of the American government to create a unipolar system have created barriers to China's growth and its involvement as an active actor in international affairs. Undoubtedly, its status has improved because of its economic growth, but it is still far behind acting as a fully-fledged global power despite its UNSC veto power. The United States has used its economic power and influence to limit China's economic and military advancement, a parameter in China's limited political influence in global affairs. Briefly, China also sees itself as a victim of the existing international system, which creates barriers to its achievement of a desired status. In conclusion, for different reasons, Iran, India, and Russia have strong reasons for grievances against the international system, shared also by China.

Sharing Compatible Views about Regional and International Affairs

Iran, India, and Russia have common, close, or similar views about many major international and regional issues. As mentioned earlier, they are all dissatisfied with the American effort to create a unipolar international system in which all of them will become marginalized, if not forced to accept practical subjugation. As aspiring powers, newcomers and old ones, their status as regional powers and their interests can only be preserved and respected in a multipolar international system where each of them can be a pole with all its merits and responsibilities. However, the achievement of that objective requires their collaboration to ensure its existence and continuity. That requires their resistance to any effort by the United States to dominate their regions and to exclude them from or at least to minimize their influence there. On the one hand, this common objective has been translated into their joint objection to the expansion of American political and military power especially in Asia, the Middle East, and Eastern Europe.

The Iranian-Russian opposition to the eastward expansion of NATO has been a well-known example of this case. On the other hand, their shared objective has manifested itself in their common policy in many security affairs in Central Asia, the Caucasus, and Afghanistan. These are regions of importance to all of them not only for security considerations, but also for economic and political reasons. Consequently, Iran, India, and Russia have all sought to cooperate in those regions by pursuing the same broad policy toward its security and by trying to prevent a disastrous scenario for all of them (i.e., the total American domination of those regions). This has occurred despite their competition and even conflicts over economic issues such as the division of the oil-rich Caspian Sea. The latter has been a major source of irritation in relations between Iran and Russia. Their backing of the Northern Alliance in Afghanistan and the Iranian/Russian efforts toward ending the civil war in Tajikistan and maintaining its peace since the June 1997 peace accord are two widely known recent examples of their security cooperation.

Despite its extensive economic ties with the United States, China is also against U.S. domination in the international system. That scenario would prevent China, a rising regional power with global ambitions, from consolidating its power as a nuclear state in world affairs, while turning it over time into an appendage of U.S. power. Despite its UNSC permanent membership, China does not have a corresponding economic and military strength to pursue its global objectives. Unless it overcomes these deficiencies, its current status as a UNSC member will not be a strong guarantee for eminent status for that country. Like Iran, India, and Russia, China is concerned about instability in its neighboring Afghanistan and Central Asia and favors peace and stability there. The American domination of these neighboring country and region and its military presence in China's vicinity are also reasons for concerns for the Chinese whom a growing number of Americans see as a future economic and military threat. As a recent example, Thomas Woodrow, a former senior China analyst at the Defense Intelligence Agency in Washington D.C., reflected this view in an August 2002 article published by an American think tank, the Jamestown Foundation. Thus, he held:

The recent release of two U.S. government studies on China—the Pentagon's annual report of Chinese military strength, and the findings of the Congressional U.S.-China Security Review Commission—should come as a wake-up call to those who craft U.S. China policy. Many of those who are engaged in China policy or who invest there remain blithely ignorant of Chinese goals to replace the United States as the reigning world power. This is especially true of those who continue to pour billions of dollars of investment into the Chinese fata morgana of future profit. These two studies make it quite clear that the [People's Republic of China] is rapidly emerging as a future threat to U.S. political and economic aspirations.[14]

Sharing a Sense of Threat

The three regional powers and China also share a sense of threat. To a varying extent and in different forms, various internal and external factors have created threats, which make them all vulnerable politically and economically, while endangering their national security.

Compared to the other three states, Russia faces the most serious and extensive internal threats. Emerging right after the collapse of the Soviet Union, the threats have taken a variety of violent and nonviolent forms. Undoubtedly, the most contributing factor to the rise of internal threats was the sudden fall of the Soviet Union. The latter opened Pandora's box, letting all sorts of forces of instability emerge and expand. As a nonpolitical factor, the sudden increase in violent criminal activities such as drug-trafficking, armed robbery, and assaults has been a major source of concern for the Russian government. In 1995, the year for which statistics exist, 36.9 percent of the Russians living in Moscow were victimized by crime.[15] The poor economic situation has created a ripe situation for the expansion of violent crimes. The Russian authorities have failed to curb such crimes because of a variety of problems ranging from lack of police expertise to a severe shortage of funds. The growth of violent crimes has remained a serious problem to this date as reflected in a high number of drug addicts estimated at between 3 and 4 million in 2001, an indication of the wide scale of drug-trafficking.[16]

Regarding the political source of internal threats, in the 1990s the severe conflicts and rivalry among the numerous large and small political parties were a major source of concern for the Russian government. Their activities made contributions to a chaotic political situation in the post–Soviet era. The gradual strengthening of the Russian government has changed that situation in favor of a more predictable and stable political environment. President Boris Yeltsin and his successor President Vladimir Putin have managed to create a consensus among the Russian political elite, while muting their most undesirable ones through a visible resort to a high-handed policy toward the opposition groups, peaceful and violent alike. However, the expansion of extremist groups, namely a spectrum of racist, fascist, and Nazi groups promoting and demanding a Russian chauvinist and racist policy toward domestic and foreign affairs, has become a growing threat to Russia's stability. President Putin expressed his concern about that threat in his April 2002 State of the Nation Address.[17] If this trend continues, it will create a major problem not only for the Russian political system, but also for other countries, especially Russia's neighbors. The latter may well become the first target of any aggressive policy of a Russian government dominated or influenced by extremist groups.

Apart from this factor, as a multi-ethnic country with large non-Russian ethnic minorities, ethnic conflicts have been a major destabilizing force in

Russia. It has taken the form of demands for an autonomous status within the framework of the Russian Federation (e.g., Tataristan) to an outright demand for independence from Russia. Chechnya has been a well-known case of the latter, which has created major difficulties for the Russian government since 1991. Its inability to end the decade-long armed conflict and to restore fully Russia's authority over the breakaway republic has been a major source of embarrassment, while undermining its power and prestige both at home and abroad. The Russian extensive military operation of 1994–1996 failed to make the republic accept the authority of Moscow. The second operation, which began in 1999, has not changed the situation, although it has destroyed most of Chechnya. Four years after its initiation, the Chechen militants have not been uprooted as hoped and planned by the Russian authorities. Resorting to small-scale hit-and-run operations, they have inflicted heavy casualties on the Russian troops who control cities in the morning and seek shelter at fortified military bases at night. As claimed in October 2002 by the Russian forces' commander in Chechnya, Col. Gen. Vladimir I. Moltenskoi, their killing of 10,000 to 13,000 Chechen fighters and their loss of 4,500 troops have not resolved the conflict whose end is anybody's guess.[18]

The continuation of the armed independence movement in Chechnya has created major difficulties for Russia in two ways. It has imposed a heavy cost on the Russian government at the time when it faces numerous economic problems, including severe financial ones. Economic problems aside, the continuation of the Chechen movement despite the Russian government's massive military operation has been alarming, not only because of its implication for Chechnya itself, but also because of its impact on other Russian republics housing ethnic minorities. The first two "ideal" candidates are Chechnya's neighboring republics of Daghistan and Inghushetia. The two republics have experienced a variety of armed conflicts "exported" by Chechens to their republics, as well as a gradual rising discontent among their peoples.[19]

Beside the internal threats, Russia is concerned about its encirclement by (active or potential) hostile, unpredictable, or unreliable states. This is a serious external threat at a time when the Russian government is unable to deal with major hostilities along its long borders as a result of its numerous domestic problems and limited available resources. Currently, Russia is not facing an immediate external threat endangering its national security. However, there are clear signs of future threats on the part of different foreign actors. Without any question, the NATO eastward expansion has been a major source of concern for the Russians. The disintegration of the Soviet empire resulted in the sudden disappearance of the Warsaw Pact. The fall of the pro-Soviet regimes of the eastern European countries pushed them out of Russia's sphere of influence as they all opted to seek extensive ties with the Western countries. This development was initially translated into a loss of market for Russia, but not a major security concern for its leaders. At that time, Russia's interest in close ties with the Western countries reciprocated by them removed from the Russian political scene the prevailing Soviet era's views of the West as the main source of security threat.

However, the interest of the eastern European countries to join NATO has changed the situation. Although the hostile Cold War type of relations no longer exists, Russia's hoped-for close and extensive ties with its ex-enemies are yet to be materialized. The Western countries have shown in their pattern of relations that they have no intention to view Russia as an equal friendly state. Contrary to the Russians' hope, the meager financial assistance provided to Russia in the form of loans, grants, and investments has clearly shown that the Western countries have no interest in providing Russia with a Marshall Plan-type of assistance. Beside low foreign investments in Russia, this reluctance to help has also been reflected in low foreign development assistance per capita for Russia. In 1999 for which comparable statistics are available, with a population of 146.2 million, Russia received $1,816.3 million in official development assistance, while Poland with a population of 38.6 million received $983.8 million.[20] This lack of interest has been a major external factor in prolonging the Russian economic problems inherited from the Soviet era, which have been worsened by the transitional process from its state-controlled economy to a type of market economy. The availability of generous financial packages to former Soviet bloc members in eastern Europe now joined NATO such as Poland has clearly indicated the Western countries' interest in a weak Russia. While those packages may not address all their problems, they are large enough to make a significant positive impact on their economies.

In such a situation, the membership of the eastern European states in NATO is worrisome for Russia. That development removes the buffer between Russia and western Europe when the latter and Russia's former allies seem unreliable friends despite their current peaceful relations with Russia. Thus, the gradual degeneration of former allies into unreliable and unfriendly neighbors, who could easily turn into enemies in the future, creates realistic grounds for a security fear for the Russians. They have become very vulnerable to external threats because of their poor economy. Given the depth of their domestic problems, the Russians require a few decades of nonstop growth to address their extensive economic and social problems, which have significantly reduced both their conventional and nuclear military capabilities. The NATO eastward expansion has therefore become a major source of concern for Russia. The NATO membership of Poland, Hungary, and the Czech Republic in 1999 both angered and concerned Russia, although it did not use the occasion to open a new round of hostility. Such reaction was not a sign of the unimportance of the development, but an indicator of Russia's inability to put up a fight. The new round of NATO recruitment, which will consider the membership request of Russia's other ex-Soviet allies, will certainly lay the ground for an era of mistrust and hostility between Russia and NATO. The membership of other eastern European countries will turn NATO into a neighbor of Russia. This is an undesirable and potentially dangerous scenario, which the Russians have tried to prevent since 1991.

In May 2002, the official expansion of NATO-Russian relations during the Reykjavik meeting seemed more like a face-saving measure for Russia than an attempt to address its concerns of being squeezed by potentially hostile NATO states. According to the NATO-Russian agreement reached during the meeting, NATO grants Russia an equal partner status on "discussions and actions with the nineteen NATO members on a variety of issues, including non-proliferation, military cooperation and civilian emergency planning."[21] However, the nineteen NATO member states, including the United States, "will preserve full control over membership in the alliance and over core military decisions and the use of allied troops to defend member nations, and they can vote to restrict discussion of any topic they choose."[22] Apparently, the latter gave Russia a mainly ceremonial degree of representation in NATO without giving it any say in the internal affairs of NATO, including its future enlargements.

Apart from NATO, Russia is also concerned about the gradual emergence of the European Union (EU) as an aspiring superpower. At the moment, the EU is far from a coherent organization capable of acting as a united bloc, an unlikely possibility in the near future. However, there is no question that its so-called heavyweights, especially France and Germany, are striving to turn it into a fully functional global power, a status that neither country can achieve on its own for a predictably long period of time. As the EU enlargement has also taken an eastward direction, the planned gradual membership of Russia's former allies and republics will prepare grounds for tension between the EU and Russia, despite the fact that the Russians have been trying to expand their ties with the EU. In the summer of 2002, this became evident in the rise of conflict between Moscow and Brussels over a decision of Poland and one of Russia's former Baltic republics to impose visa on the Russians living in Kalinengrad, a Russian enclave surrounded by the two countries. In tune with EU regulations, the two soon-to-become EU members announced their future imposition of visa on all the Russians living in Kalinengrad who wished to travel to Russia mainland via rail passing through their countries. As many of its residents travel back and forth to Russia on a regular basis for reasons such as visiting their families, the imposition of a visa requirement will certainly put financial and bureaucratic barriers on them after 2004 when Poland and Lithuania join the EU. A predictable result will be the denial of easy access to Russia to many of them, while weakening Russia's ties with its territory now apart from the mainland as a result of the Soviet Union's disintegration.

The EU insists on imposing visa for two reasons. First, given the high unemployment rate in Kalinengrad, Poland and Lithuania could face an inflow of the enclave's Russians in search of employment. The economic benefits of EU membership would probably make the two countries especially attractive for those Russians. Second, the absence of a visa requirement for EU nationals travelling in the EU countries will enable the Russians to travel easily in the EU countries through Poland and Lithuania unless a visa requirement prevents them from doing so. In early November 2002, Russia and the EU reached an agreement to solve the issue in a manner acceptable to both sides, such as issuing low-fee visas for the Kalinengrad Russians.[23] Yet, it is not clear how such an arrangement will solve the problem permanently as the better economic environment in the two new EU members may make them too tempting to be resisted by the Russians living in the economically depressed Kalinengrad. Irritations, if not conflicts, between Russia and the EU over the free access of those Russians to the Russian mainland will probably be a predictable scenario in the future. Since many future EU members are also NATO applicants or members, the eastward EU expansion will predictably create more clashes of interests, reinforcing Russia's fear of a total encirclement by hostile states.

As will be discussed in detail, the increasing American military presence in Russia's proximity is yet another source of external threat for Russia. Before the American war in Afghanistan, this was mainly a function of the NATO eastward expansion with a practical increase in the American military presence in those countries, a "natural" outcome of its status as the largest NATO state. The latter has been a concern for Russia for its creating a threat along Russia's western borders with Europe. The significant American military presence in the Pacific Ocean such as in Japan has been another concern for Russia as it shares a long border with the ocean in short distance from Japan. Yet another concern has been the existence of American troops in South Korea to deter any North Korean attack on that country. They pose a potential threat to the Russian Pacific region as North Korea shares a short border with Russia.

However, since late 2001, the American military operation in Afghanistan has suddenly changed the situation in a vast area along Russia's southern borders. The deployment of American troops in Afghanistan and in some Central Asian and Caucasian countries (Georgia, Kyrgyzstan, and Uzbekistan) and certain recent developments have led to a significant increase in the American military presence along or close to Russia's southern borders. Those developments are the expansion of military ties between the Americans and other Caucasian and Central Asian states in the form of receiving over-flight and emergency landing (Kazakhstan and Turkmenistan) or the sale of arms and providing military training (e.g., Azerbaijan and Georgia). Given the American military presence along other Russian borders, its growing presence along its southern borders has been a source of anxiety for Moscow.

Although not a current threat, China, which shares a very long border with Russia in the south, has been a "traditional" source of threat to Russia since the early 1960s. The skirmishes along the Sino-Soviet borders in the 1960s over territorial disputes did not lead to a full-scale war in the Soviet era. The rapprochement between the two countries in the last decade of the Soviet Union eased tensions and made their common borders peaceful, a situation lasting to this date. In the post–Soviet era, the rapid expansion of economic relations, including selling Russian arms to China, has consolidated their peaceful and friendly relations. However, in the long run such relations may not last, given the existence of various historical reasons for mistrust and hostility between the two neighbors dating back to the nineteenth century. Currently and for a long time in the foreseeable future, the two countries will not seek conflicts as they both need a long period of peace to address their numerous transitional problems. However, their desire to establish themselves as global powers and to seek an upper hand in Asia and the Pacific Ocean will create tensions in their relations once at least one of them feels strong enough to challenge the other. For this reason, Russia is concerned about its full encirclement in the future when China turns into an aggressive rival power. This makes the growing American military presence along its borders even more threatening.

Unlike Russia, Iran does not suffer from apparent internal threats. Its Islamic regime has suppressed all major opposition groups capable of posing a serious challenge to its authority. Nor does Iran have any independence movement challenging the authority of the central government and the stability of the country. Hence there is no immediate source of internal problem. However, the political developments since the ascension to power of President Mohammad Khatami have indicated the existence of a growing popular movement demanding a fundamental change in the political system, which has failed to meet many aspirations of the Iranians. The current president came to power on a clear reformist agenda in 1997 and for the second time in 2001 when the majority of voters cast their ballots to support a peaceful and gradual transition to a democratic society. However, the Iranian political system has remained undemocratic, despite limited and mainly superficial changes, which have brought a little personal freedom and a fragile freedom of press undermined by the Iranian judiciary in a "legal" manner. This is a result of a constant power struggle between the reformist and conservative factions of the regime. The latter has prevented the full implementation of reforms intended to remove some of the social (e.g., severe restrictions on women and youth) and political (e.g., absence of political rights for individuals) barriers, while addressing some of the major economic problems (e.g., the sluggish growth and growing unemployment). More important, this is a consequence of the limited objectives of the reformist agenda. The reformers have aimed at dealing with some of the problems, which make governing the country difficult. They may also undermine the very basis of the Islamic regime by eroding its legitimacy.

Hence, the reformist objective of preserving the political system in its totality, while addressing some of its malfunctions, has limited the scope of the envisaged reforms to the extent possible within the existing political system. For this simple reason, the reformist agenda is way behind the popular demand for a fundamental change in a political system, which has failed to meet its people's aspirations. In 2002, after five years of "reform," the overwhelming majority of the promised changes (e.g., personal, social, and political freedoms, justice, equality, and democracy) have remained unfulfilled. The Iranians seem to have come to the conclusion that the Islamic system is not reformable, and they show signs of losing interest in the "reformist" faction. As reflected in a government-conducted opinion poll released in late 2002, 90 percent of the Iranians are dissatisfied with the existing religious regime and its interpretation of Islam as the governing ideology of the state.[24] Moreover, they disagree with its conduct of foreign policy. This is evident in another opinion poll conducted at the request of the Iranian parliament's foreign affairs committee by three governmental polling organizations to ensure its reliability. According to the poll, 74.7 percent of Iranians supported negotiations with the United States to normalize ties if such ties served Iranian interests.[25]

As the economic problems expand and popular dissatisfaction with the state of affairs increases, there is every indication that Iranian society is heading toward a process of regime change. In October 2002, a reformer member of Iranian parliament disillusioned with the reformist faction, Ghasem Sholeh-sadi, described the inevitability of this change in a radio interview as he stated:

The disillusionment of the Iranians with all factions of the Islamic regime, which have controlled the government since 1979, including the reformers who now control both the executive and legislative powers, has paved the way for the rise of a popular movement outside the Islamic political system. You could call it the new reformist movement or the third force. The rising movement has certain demands, which are very simple as they are the demands of the Iranians unfulfilled by different factions of the Islamic regime since its creation. These are freedom, democracy, justice and equality.[26]

The emergence of a movement for a regime change has been evident in the demand for secularism among the well-known reformers now outside the political system. A famous example is the release of a "manifest of republicanism" by Akbar Ganji. A pro-Khatami journalist, his efforts to disclose extensive human rights abuses, including serial killing of anti-regime activists by the Iranian security forces, finally led to his arrest and trial on fabricated charges in 2000. While in prison, Mr. Ganji released his "manifest" to prove the necessity of a secular republic, while explaining why President Khatami's reformist efforts are hopeless as they would only perpetuate the existing undemocratic system.[27] The manifest has provoked a debate both inside and outside the in-power reformist faction.

Apart from that, there has been a growing expression of dissent among members of the civil society, including lawyers and journalists. They have demanded accountability of the ruling elite in addition to an end to human rights abuses and social and political restrictions. In September 2002, the arrest and secret trial of a number of well-known lawyers, including Mr. Nasser Zarafshan, a lawyer who defended the family of those who had been killed by secret execution squads, is a well-known case. Various Western news media reported the arrests, and human rights groups such as Amnesty International condemned them in the same month.[28] Finally, the growing labor disputes and student protests in the form of strikes, demonstrations, meetings, and vigils in main cities such as Tehran, Tabriz, Isfahan, and Hamedan have also reflected the expansion of dissatisfaction among the Iranian labor force. In November 2002, the sudden eruption of student activities in protest to the arrest and sentencing to death of a university professor, Hashem Aghajary, for his speech criticizing the Iranian clergy reflected the depth of dissatisfaction with the status quo. The rapidly growing protests began with a demand for his release only to change direction and demand fundamental changes in the political system. The students showed their disillusionment with the reformist faction by targeting the entire governing elite, conservatives and reformers alike, in their slogans and by demanding the resignation of President Khatami.[29]

Although a regime change in Iran seems inevitable, it is difficult to predict what form this process will take. The Iranians have paid a heavy personal, social, economic, political, and international price for the 1979 revolution and its resulting political system, which has resorted to undemocratic means to implement its polices regardless of its people's disapproval. Despite a repressive regime in power, certain factors suggest that there is an evident desire among the majority of the Iranians favoring democratic means for popular expression of dissent. They include the emergence of numerous forums of popular participation in the political process (e.g., NGOs and nonpolitical interest groups), an impressive increase in the quantity and the quality of printed media, massive popular participation in elections, and the election of reformist candidates with a large number of votes. If this trend continues, a peaceful and gradual process of change through democratic means such as referenda and pushed by popular pressure will be the preferential method of regime change for the majority of Iranians. In June 2003 the university students who demonstrated in Tehran and many other Iranian cities for several days demanded a referundum on the desired type of political system. They clearly expressed their opposition to the ruling theocracy, while demanding a secular democracy. However, apart from this likely popular preference as evident in the mentioned student protests, the reaction of the Islamic regime toward a popular demand for regime change will determine the exact form of the process. A zero-tolerance approach will most probably radicalize any popular movement to make the people interested in violence as the only way to induce a regime change. Regardless of its final form, the emerging popular movement for change will make the Islamic regime vulnerable domestically. In turn, this weakness will make it more vulnerable to external threats.

As for external threats, Iran faces serious challenges. In practice, it is very close to becoming fully encircled by hostile or potentially hostile countries. In the south, the Iranian government has established peaceful relations with its Persian Gulf Arab states, including expanding economic relations. In particular, Iran's ties with its main enemies in the 1980s, Saudi Arabia and Kuwait, have become very close, friendly, and extensive. In 2002, for instance, many Bahraini, Kuwaiti, and Saudi high officials paid visits to Tehran such as Saudi Minister of Interior Amir Nayef bin Abdulaziz (April), Saudi Minister of Foreign Affairs Prince Saud al-Faisal (August), Emir of Bahrain Shikh Hamad bin Essa Al-Khaliefe (August), and Kuwaiti Minister of Defence Shikh Jaber Mobarak (September).[30] Apart from political and economic affairs, Iranian relations with these two important Persian Gulf countries also include security cooperation. As a recent example, in 2002 Iran extradited to Saudi Arabia many al-Qadea suspects who had crossed the border into Iran from Afghanistan and Pakistan after the Americans began their operation in Afghanistan.[31]

Despite these peaceful and friendly relations, Iran still faces a serious potential threat, not from these countries, but from the American forces stationed there. This is a "natural" negative result of Iranian-American troubled relations. The United States has kept its military bases in Saudi Arabia and Kuwait since the end of the Persian Gulf War of 1991. The headquarters of the American Fifth Fleet is in Bahrain, while the Americans have stationed troops in Oman and Qatar. The latter has become the headquarters of the American forces in the Persian Gulf. While hosting tens of thousands of American military personnel, the Kuwaitis' uncertain consent to any American use of their military bases in case of war with Iraq convinced the Americans in 2002 to move the headquarters of their forces in the Persian Gulf from Kuwait to Qatar. The UAE has also granted overflight and emergency landing to the American forces, although it does not host them. Given this situation, the American forces are stationed along the Oman Sea and the Persian Gulf southern coastline from where they could technically launch attacks on Iran located across the water should Iranian-American relations reach a very hostile level.

Iran's southern border is vulnerable, but its western border is not any safer. The Iranians owe this situation to their uncertain ties with their western neighbors, Iraq and Turkey. The former has been a traditional enemy of Iran since the 1960s, which invaded Iran in 1980 to engage it in a devastating eight-year war of attrition. With the UN mediation in 1988, the two countries ended the war without concluding a peace treaty to settle all their differences. As surprising as it may sound, the two countries have yet to address certain basic issues fifteen years after the war ended. For example, there are still hundreds of Iranian POWs in Iraq in addition to thousands of Iranian civilians kidnapped by the advancing Iraqi forces at the early stage of the war. Furthermore, the UN resolution of 1990 identifying Iraq as the instigator of the war and demanding it to pay to Iran $100 billion in reparation is yet to be implemented. Iran and Iraq host each other's armed opposition groups, a natural behavior given the depth of the two countries' mistrust and hostility toward each other. Although they are not involved in a military conflict, they do not have normal relations with each other. Instead, a fragile no-war no-peace situation has been in place since 1988. Their current relations are far from stable, predictable, and friendly. However, their future relations will be even more threatening, given the American occupation of Iraq and Washington's plan to install a pro-American regime in Baghdad and to station large numbers of troops in Iraq for a long time. Undoubtedly, a pro-American Iraq hosting American forces will pose a serious threat to Iran if Iranian-American relations remain estranged.

In particular, that situation would be a horrible security scenario for Iran given the heavy military presence of the Americans in Turkey, a western neighbor of Iran and a northern neighbor of Iraq. As a NATO member and an American ally, Turkey hosts a large number of American military personnel stationed in a variety of army, airforce, and reconnaissance bases. Their sheer existence in a neighboring country is a source of justifiable concern for the Iranian regime. Yet, the geographical location of some of them, such as the Dyar Baker airforce base and a few reconnaissance centers close to the Turkish-Iranian border, creates a special sense of insecurity in Iran. Keeping this situation in mind, while Iranian-Turkish relations have been peaceful and lacked major upheavals since 1997, the existence of American forces in Turkey creates a major potential threat to Iran's national security.

To this, one should add the potential of a hostile Turkish policy toward Iran, which would make the situation particularly alarming. Turkey's rivalry with Iran over political influence and economic gains in two regions of importance to the two neighbors, the Caucasus and Central Asia, has created grounds for dissatisfaction both in Tehran and Ankara. As the Americans have sought to stop Iranian advancements in those regions, the Turkish and American policy toward Iran and those regions coincide. For that matter, Turkey has become the main regional beneficiary of the American policy aimed at minimizing Iran's involvement in the development and export of the Caspian Sea region's oil and natural gas resources. In spite of Iran's offering the shortest, cheapest, and safest export route for Caspian oil and gas, the Americans have created obstacles to its use. Instead, they have promoted a long, highly costly, and unsafe pipeline, the Baku-Tiblisi-Ceyhan pipeline, despite a lack of interest on the part of many American oil companies developing most of the Caspian oil and gas fields.[32]

The pipeline has been a source of irritation and anger in Iranian-Turkish relations since 1994. At that time, the pipeline idea emerged as a way to bypass both Iran and Russia for the long-term Caspian oil exports. In September 2002, after years of delay, the beginning of its construction only ignited resentment not only in Iran but also in Russia, another major loser. It is not certain whether the pipeline will be constructed as planned to become operational in late 2004. Nor is it certain whether, if its operators find a way to ensure its safety, an uncertain bid given the worsening of the security situation in the Caucasus, it is going to be an economically sensible means for exporting Caspian oil. Among other factors such as the high cost of ensuring its safety and of its maintenance, the reluctance of other Caspian oil exporters (i.e., Kazakhstan and Turkmenistan) to use it as their main means of oil export will make the cost of export through the pipeline very high. The June 2002 Russian-Kazakh agreements by which Kazakhstan made itself committed to use the available Russian pipeline for the export of about 90 percent of its current oil exports will not leave much for the Baku-Tiblisi-Ceyhan pipeline even if they decide to use it.[33] Accordingly, the agreement provided for the transit of Kazakh oil via the Russian route of Atyrau-Samara and Makhachkala-Tikhoretsk-Novorossiisk for fifteen years.[34] The volume of transit can not be less than 17.5 million tons per year.[35]

However, the beginning of the mentioned pipeline's construction has contributed to mistrust between Iran and Turkey. This is only partly because of an irritating pipeline's objective to weaken the Iranian economy by denying it a share of the lucrative Caspian oil business. As a prelude to its construction, Turkey's refusal to keep buying Iranian natural gas in 2002 after many months of importing further damaged the two countries' relations. Iran invested hundreds of millions of dollars in constructing a pipeline to export gas to Turkey in the late 1990s. After about two years of delay, Turkey finally constructed its part and began to import gas in December 2001. In June 2002, it suddenly stopped buying gas on the grounds of its "poor quality." However, it was more than clear that three factors promoted this decision. One was Turkey's deep economic problems that resulted in a much lower demand in natural gas and a severe shortage of funds for imports. Another was Turkey's overestimation of its gas requirements in the 1990s based on a very unrealistic assumption of economic growth, which never materialized. That led to its conclusion of gas pipeline agreements with Iran and Russia, while signing other contracts with Azerbaijan, Turkmenistan, Egypt, and Nigeria. Contrary to the expectations, Turkey faced a very serious economic crisis and a large shrinkage of GDP in 2000 and 2001 reflected in part in its foreign debt of over $117.5 billion in 2002.[36] Finally, Turkey has long been under pressure by the Americans to stop its energy agreements with Iran. The latter would undermine the American efforts to push for the Baku-Tiblisi-Ceyhan pipeline based partly on the unreliability of the Iranian export route. As well, such agreements would be contrary to the American efforts to weaken Iran's economy. As part of their policy of helping Turkey, while decreasing its interest in Iran's gas, in late 2002 the Americans pressured the Russians to decrease by 9 percent the price of their gas sold to Turkey via the undersea Blue Line pipeline.[37]

The severe economic difficulties created a major financial burden on the Turks to pay for their imported gas from Iran. In such a situation, they took the opportunity to stop their imports to please the Americans and to relieve their financial burden to some extent, while finding an excuse not to abide by the terms of gas agreement with Iran (i.e., take or pay). The Turks hoped that they would be able to force the Iranians to decrease the gas price as they could not afford keeping their gas pipeline idle after spending hundreds of millions of dollars on its construction. Keeping that in mind, in October 2002, Iran, which cannot afford a hostile Turkey, agreed to revise the agreement to decrease the gas price and to exempt the Turks from their commitment to buy 9 billion cubic meters of gas annually.[38] As both sides adhered to a policy of not disclosing the details of the agreement, including the new agreed gas price, evidence suggests that the Iranians had to accept at least a 9 percent discount to match the Russian discount.

If the southern and western neighbors are worrisome, Iran's northern and eastern ones are not any better. In the post–September 11 era, the Americans have deployed their troops in Central Asia and the Caucasus, both neighboring Iran in the north. Of course, those troops are stationed in Georgia, Uzbekistan, and Kyrgyzstan, three countries with no common borders with Iran. However, they are close enough to Iran to be used in any American military confrontation with that country or as a means of exercising pressure on the Iranians. As reflected in a series of military cooperation agreements between Azerbaijan and the United States in March and April 2002, the latter's growing military ties with Iran's neighboring Azerbaijan has been a clear source of alarm for the Iranian government.[39] The Americans have aimed at helping Azerbaijan beef up its military force to face any Iranian future challenge. Given the existence of various sources of tension in Iranian-Azeri relations, including major disagreements over the division of the Caspian Sea and thus the ownership of its offshore oil fields, there is a realistic ground for future conflicts and even confrontations. In such a case, the Americans and even Turkey could be dragged into the conflict nilly willy. A 2001 case substantiates this statement.

Disputes over the ownership of certain Caspian offshore oil fields between Iran and Azerbaijan and between Azerbaijan and Turkmenistan reached an unprecedented hostile stage in 2001. In that year, Iran and Turkmenistan accused Azerbaijan of its illegal development and operation of certain disputed oil fields to which all three states have ownership claims. They also accused Azerbaijan of its efforts to develop other disputed oil fields with the assistance of foreign oil companies. Furthermore, they accused Azerbaijan of violating their territorial waters with its military and non-military vessels, while Azerbaijan accused them of the same violations. On one occasion, the Iranian navy allegedly forced an Azeri oil exploration ship to leave a disputed oil field.[40] While Iran evaluated the incident as a minor issue in Iranian-Azeri relations, Azerbaijan considered it a major event endangering its territorial rights and economic interests.

In its aftermath, certain developments contributed to the escalation of tension in the Caspian region. One was Turkey's dispatch of a small number of fighter jets to Azerbaijan under the pretext of participating in a previously arranged air show.[41] Azerbaijan's official and unofficial references to Turkey's move as a clear sign of its determination to defend the Azeris in any future confrontation with Iran offset Turkey's official statements downgrading the move's significance. Of course, the Turks made sure that the "air show" left no doubt about their taking sides with the Azeris. Another development was the simultaneous official visit of Turkey's chairman of the joint chief of staff to Azerbaijan (General Hossein Kivrigoglou), which was treated in the same manner by the Turks and the Azeris. Not only did the two developments create tension in Iran's ties with Azerbaijan, they provoked the disapproval of other littoral states and particularly of Russia and Turkmenistan. Finally, the sale of two American military boats to Azerbaijan added fuel to its conflicts with Iran and Turkmenistan.[42] The two countries expressed deep concern about the transaction, which they portrayed as a threat to their national security and a provocative act leading to an arms race. In particular, Turkmenistan's reaction was very strong and included its revelation of its purchase of Ukrainian military boats, which in turn provoked a harsh Azeri reaction.[43]

Turkmenistan, another neighbor of Iran in the north, has been on good terms with Iran since its independence. Iranian-Turkmen bilateral relations have expanded in all fields, including military. Not only is Turkmenistan a major regional economic partner of Iran, it receives military assistance from that country as provided by a 1994 agreement.[44] However, Turkmenistan's granting overflight and emergency landing rights to the Americans should have created anxiety for the Iranian government, although it is very unlikely that the Turkmen government will allow an American military attack on Iran from its territory.

The military presence of the Americans in Afghanistan and Pakistan, Iran's eastern neighbors, has almost completed Iran's encirclement by American troops. The consolidation of the American political and military influence along Iran's eastern neighbors will create a major security threat for Tehran. However, that scenario can happen only if the current pattern of alliance between Pakistan and the United States continues. As well, it can happen if the Americans manage to turn the existing pro-American, but extremely weak, government of Hamid Karzai into a strong central government in full control over the entire country. The latter would be a rather difficult task at least in the short run, unless the American government makes itself committed to and dedicates a significant amount of resources and efforts to that objective.

India has a variety of domestic sources of threat. In fact, it has faced most of them ever since its independence in 1947. A few decade-long armed "revolutionary" activities by left-wing extremist groups generically referred to as Naxalites have posed a security challenge to the Indian government, forcing it to fight with armed guerrillas in at least five states (i.e., Bihar, Uttar Pradesh, Uttaranchal, West Bengal, and Sikkim). Apart from this limited security threat, India is concerned about three major domestic threats. A well-known one is the status of Kashmir, which pitted India against Pakistan right after independence.[45] The war between the two newly independent neighbors did not solve the problem as it left a part of Kashmir under control of each side. To find a peaceful solution to the conflict, a UN resolution provided for a referendum to settle the status of Kashmir by the Kashmiris. However, the Indian government has since refused to allow it as it might result in two unfavorable scenarios for India, given the majority of the Kashmiris are Muslim. There would be either a demand for unification with Pakistan or a demand for independence from both India and Pakistan to create an independent state of Kashmir as a result of the unification of the two parts of Kashmir now under India and Pakistan. Thus, India's refusal to allow a referendum has provided grounds for decades of instability in that part of India, the result of the radicalization of the Kashmiris living under Indian rule. Over time, the emergence of armed groups generically known as *jihadis* advocating violence as the only means for "liberating" Kashmir has left thousands of deaths on both sides of the conflict, including many non-belligerent civilians. The fact that India has accused the Pakistani government of backing the Kashmiri militants called "terrorists" by the Indians and "freedom fighters" by the Pakistanis has not changed the significance of the conflict in Kashmir as a major domestic source of threat to India's national security.

Especially over the last two decades, the rise of a separatist movement in Punjab has been another major source of domestic threat for the Indian government. Punjab is inhabited mainly by Sikhs, and there has been a movement advocating the secession of Punjab from India and the creation of a Sikh state called *Khalistan*. The movement has consisted of many large and small groups working toward that end through peaceful as well as violent means. Regardless of the means those groups advocate to achieve their objective, their movement has been a clear threat to the Indian state and particularly to its territorial integrity. Within this framework, the activities of violent Sikh groups have been especially alarming. The latter became particularly active in the 1980s and in the most part of the 1990s turning Punjab and many other Indian states and cities, including Delhi itself, into a battleground. Numerous attacks and counterattacks by the Sikh armed groups and the Indian security forces on each other, as well as massive abuses of human rights by both sides, including the assassination by the Sikh extremists of many moderate Sikhs opposing violence, painted that period. The 1984 assassination of the late Indira Gandhi, then the Indian prime minister, indicated the depth of the Sikh violence. Thanks to a massive suppression of militants, Punjab has become a more peaceful state these days, although the secessionist movement still exists. Since the root causes of the movement (e.g., dissatisfaction with the Indian state in Punjab) have not yet been addressed, many factors, including changes in local, regional, and international situations will likely contribute to the reemergence of the movement in the future.

Finally, sectarian violence has been yet another major domestic source of concern for the Indian government since independence. In fact, it emerged years prior to independence in the form of conflicts between Hindu and Muslim leaders of India's independence movement. On occasions, such conflicts took the form of violent clashes between their supporters, which created enough mistrust and hostility between the two communities to prepare social grounds for the partition of India into Hindu-dominated India and Muslim-dominated Pakistan. Sectarian violence has since continued on the on-and-off basis as major cities like Delhi have become the scene of bloody clashes between Hindu and Muslim extremists agitating their respective followers and ordinary people to launch violent acts against the neighborhoods of the opposite religious sects. Unsurprisingly, such acts always provoke violence in revenge by the victimized sect, which turn major cities into battlegrounds between extremist groups. The September 2002 bloody attacks by extremists on Muslim and Hindu communities in Gugrat is just a very recent example of an old problem.

Internal threats aside, India also faces external threats. For the Indians, geography and history have created two main external enemies, namely Pakistan and China. This is notwithstanding the fact that India has diplomatic relations with the two of them and, for the most part, its bilateral relations with them have been peaceful. China, in particular, has been a less-publicized enemy among the Indians who without a doubt view Pakistan as their main enemy. The partition of India into India and Pakistan and the process leading to it set grounds for decades of seemingly endless hostility between the two neighbors. Against that background, the issue of Kashmir has become the single major source of conflict between India and Pakistan, as it serves as a test of their statehood. First, the Indians could not accept the loss of Kashmir no matter if it would join Pakistan or not as it could set grounds for other independence movements not confined to that in Punjab. As a multiethnic country where there are hundreds of spoken languages with corresponding ethnic groups, a successful independence movement could trigger a series of similar movements elsewhere in the country. Second, the loss of Kashmir to Pakistan would be a devastating blow to the Indians who cannot accept any loss in favor of Pakistan, their archenemy.

In particular, such a development would be a great dishonor and embarrassment for the Indians who see themselves far superior to the Pakistanis. Third, as a nuclear state and an aspiring global power, such a loss would be a significant blow to its regional and international prestige.

As a result, the Indians show no serious flexibility in their approach to Kashmir. They consider it an inseparable part of their country. This approach leaves no room for a referendum and encourages violent activities supported by Pakistan. Consequently, Pakistan's desire to have the Indian-controlled Kashmir as part of its country and its providing assistance to the jihadi groups (i.e., those Kashmiri who fight to "liberate" that part of Kashmir) has been a major source of conflict between the two countries. The existence of such groups in Pakistan from where they launch their attacks on the Indian forces stationed in Kashmir have pushed the two countries toward war on many occasions. In recent years, this scenario happened twice. In 1999, during the course of the Kalgier War, a few thousand jihadis of whom some were allegedly Pakistani military personnel penetrated the Indian-controlled Kashmir and provoked skirmishes with the Indian forces there and along the ceasefire line dividing the two parts of Kashmir. That local war had the potential to lead to a full-scale war, and, as some feared, to a nuclear exchange. International mediation, including that of the United States, prevented those types of escalation at that time. In late 2001 and in early 2002, certain activities of the jihadis severely deteriorated Indian-Pakistani relations, creating a tense environment prone to a military confrontation. The Indian government blamed the Pakistani government for several armed attacks on Indian forces and a variety of terrorist attacks on civilians and politicians both in Indian-controlled Kashmir and elsewhere in India, including an attack on the Indian parliament in Delhi. Accordingly, the Pakistani government encouraged or tolerated such activities. The resulting concentration of troops along the ceasefire line created a very tense situation, which could easily escalate to a war. Concerned about a war with a damaging effect on its war in Afghanistan and also for its potential to lead to a nuclear war, the American government's mediation cooled the situation. However, it did not lead to a major withdrawal of troops on both sides of the line. In October of 2002, India's limited withdrawal of forces created hope for its possible full withdrawal if matched by Pakistan. In the first half of 2003, there was no sign of such a development.

Beside the Kashmiri issue, Pakistan's nuclear capability is yet another source of concern for India. Of course, this is a fairly new concern since both countries emerged as nuclear states only in May 1998 when Pakistan conducted nuclear tests after India did its own. Needless to say, this is a potential cause of concern, as a nuclear exchange would not serve those countries' interests, apart from the catastrophic impact on their populations. On the contrary, the expected massive destruction even in a limited nuclear war would be enough to devastate economically these two poor countries

already suffering from severe economic problems and an inadequate infrastructure. Although the existence of nuclear weapons on both sides makes
such a war a feasible scenario despite its predictable devastating impact, a
Pakistani nuclear attack on India seems a highly unlikely scenario. This is
due to the fact that India's nuclear capability is much stronger than that of
Pakistan, although the exact strength of either side's nuclear arsenal is not
clear.[46] In terms of means of delivery, India is also in a far better position as
major Pakistani cities and industrial zones are well within the range of its
short-range nuclear capable missiles, a result of geography as Pakistan is
much smaller in surface than India is. For the same geographical reasons,
Pakistan requires medium- and long-range missiles, which it lacks, to attack
many vital Indian targets. Apart from India's nuclear superiority, that country also has a much larger and more advanced conventional military force.
Therefore, Pakistan would not be a beneficiary of a nuclear or conventional
war with India. Three lost conventional wars to India in 1948, 1965, and
1971 leave no doubt in the Pakistanis' mind about the likely outcome of any
future war with their large neighbor. Nevertheless, given the strength of
Indian-Pakistani animosity, the Indians must consider the possibility of a
Pakistani nuclear attack in their security calculations.

While Pakistan is not a real long-term military threat for India because of
its numerous economic and military weaknesses, China definitely is.
Territorial disputes pushed China and India to a short bloody war along
their long joint borders in 1962, which left India as the defeated side.
China's joining the nuclear club in 1964 especially worried the Indians.
Added to India's desire to counter Pakistan's challenge enjoining the
American backing and to address its technological underdevelopment, the
Indians' fear of a growing nuclear China made them close to the Soviet
Union whose ties with China deteriorated rapidly in the 1960s. This pattern
of behavior continued throughout the Cold War era and worsened as China
emerged gradually as the major ally of Pakistan. Added to that factor,
China's much stronger, more advanced, and fast-growing economy and its
more powerful nuclear and conventional military capabilities have per-
suaded the Indians to continue their Cold War policy toward China in the
post–Cold War era. Although the two countries have not been engaged in
major conflicts and open hostilities, their ties have remained unfriendly.
This is notwithstanding the two sides' efforts to avoid confrontations, as
they both need peace and stability for a long time to find a remedy for their
underdevelopment in many fields. Unsurprisingly, the Indian officials have
repeatedly referred to China, and not to Pakistan, as the main reason for
entering the nuclear club. After the Chinese first nuclear test in 1964, the
head of the Indian Atomic Energy Commission (Homi Bhabha) announced
his country's readiness to deal with the Chinese nuclear threat in about
eighteen months.[47] The Indians repeated the Chinese threat as justification
for their developing nuclear weapons after their May 1998 tests.[48] Apart

from political incentives behind developing nuclear weapons, the latter makes sense given India's conventional military superiority to Pakistan.

In comparison to India and Russia, China does not have any major domestic force of instability. The pro-democracy movement of the late 1980s disappeared partly because of its suppression by the Chinese government, and partly because of its limited social basis (i.e., being mainly a student movement without even receiving support from the majority of the university students). Since its 1989 suppression, apart from the Chinese government's policy of zero tolerance to political dissent, many factors, including China's significant economic growth and the Chinese government's allowing more personal freedoms, have prevented the re-rise of such a movement. In the absence of a significant organized political opposition and an anti-government popular movement, expression of dissent in different forms by China's ethnic minorities has been the only significant source of domestic threat.

Surely, there are anti-government activities and movements of different extent and intensity in the minority-dominated areas. Of these, the most important ones are in Tibet and Sinkiang Province. However, they are not strong enough to threaten China's stability, in general, and to endanger the very existence of the Chinese political system, in particular, given the numerical weakness of their respective ethnic groups in proportion to China's huge population. Tibet has been more a source of international criticism and condemnation, and thus a source of irritation in China's international relations, than a security threat. However, this fact has not affected the Chinese government's pursuit of a high-handed policy toward any type of dissent in Tibet. It has also followed the same policy toward the separatist movement in Sinkiang Province. By far, the latter is a more serious security threat for the Chinese, although it has not received a lot of international attention. In particular, there has been a significant decline in reporting human rights abuses in that province since September 11. As mentioned earlier, in August 2002, the American government's adding an obscure Sinkiang separatist group to its list of terrorist organizations helped China continue its policy of suppression toward the entire dissident movement under the pretext of fighting terrorism.[49]

Regarding external threats, China's enemies are mainly potential ones. While having long-term sources of security concerns, China does not have any active enemy posing a major security threat to that country. Historically, Russia, under the Tsars and Soviet leaders, has posed security threats to China. However, Beijing has improved its relations with Moscow since the last years of the Soviet Union. The dangerous skirmishes along the Sino-Soviet border characterizing the state of relations of the two neighbors in the 1960s and hostile relations between the Soviets and the Chinese in the following decades began to disappear in the late 1980s. At that time, Soviet President Mikahil Gorbachev reached a rapprochement with the

Chinese government. Stable, predictable, and extensive ties have since prevailed. Russia is now a major trade partner of China and its main foreign source of advanced weaponry. Between 1991 and 1997 and in 2000, Russia sold, respectively, $6 billion and $2 billion worth of weapons to China.[50]

Added to this, Russia's enormous domestic problems have made the Russians preoccupied mainly with those problems whose addressing require a long period of peace. For all these reasons and its sharing China's dissatisfaction with the current international system, Russia is not a short-term threat to China's security. In the long run when the two sides are stronger economically and feel more confident, the old pattern of hostilities may well reemerge. Their political and economic rivalry in Asia where Moscow and Beijing have strategic interests should likely aggravate their conflicts.

As discussed earlier, troubled relations between India and China have turned India into a potential source of threat to China. Despite their unfriendly ties, the two neighbors have not been engaged in major conflicts, including border ones, since their 1962 short war over the disputed border areas. While the two sides view each other with suspicion, they have not since been active enemies. The memory of the short war aside, the main source of conflict between the two has been China's backing of Pakistan in its rivalry with the Soviet Union/Russia of which both have supported India. Despite its ties with Pakistan, U.S. implicit support of India by which it has sought to balance China over time has been another reason for China's taking sides with Pakistan. This has been an incentive in addition to its interest in extensive trade with that country. Although it has a numerically large military force and a nuclear capability, India is too weak militarily to pose a serious threat to China in the foreseeable future, a function of the latter's far superior nuclear and conventional military power. Similarly, India will unlikely be in a position to challenge China's military superiority for a predictably long time, owing to China's far larger, more advanced, and rapidly growing economy. This is evident in its much larger GDP in 1999 for which there are comparable statistics for India. In that year, the GDP of India and China with comparable large populations were $447.3 billion and $989.5 billion, respectively.[51] Given the much larger economic growth rate of China (9.5 percent) in the 1990s than that of India (4.1 percent) and all the likelihood of continuing its fast economic growth, that relative economic superiority grants China a significant economic capability to provide for a stronger and more advanced military force.[52] For China, a realistic and probable long-term security threat is the United States. During the last two decades, Chinese-American relations have expanded significantly, especially in the field of trade valued at over $116.4 billion in 2000 of which China's share of export to the United States was $100.1 billion.[53] These growing economic relations have created a very strong stake for China not to seek conflicts and confrontations with the United States despite its major disagreement with the latter over different issues. Against this background, the major source of tension and conflict in their bilateral relations has been the status of Taiwan. While the Americans have been committed to Taiwan's security and independence, China's efforts toward reunification with the island have created grounds for tensions in Chinese-American relations. Nevertheless, both sides, and especially China, have restrained themselves in order to prevent the escalation of their conflict over Taiwan to reach an undesirable and hostile level. Neither side sees any benefit in deteriorating their bilateral relations, including the mutually lucrative economic ties. However, as China grows stronger economically, politically, and militarily, it will likely become more assertive in pursuing its national interests. Thus, one should expect more disagreements, conflicts, and tensions between China and the United States, although major confrontations, including military ones, seem unlikely for a predictably long time. This is owing to American and Chinese heavy dependency on their bilateral trade and China's far inferior military power.

Sense of Isolation

Finally, Iran, India, and Russia share a sense of isolation. Without a doubt, they have experienced a varying degree of isolation in the international system in different forms and for a different period of time. For Iran, the 1979 revolution put the country on a path of isolation both in the region and elsewhere. Real or perceived fear of its design on its neighbors and on the "moderate" Arab states of the Middle East isolated Iran in the Persian Gulf and in the Middle East almost immediately after the revolution. Many states of those regions severed ties with Iran, while others reduced their relations to the minimum possible. Parallel to this, the Iranian regime's clear anti-Western rhetoric and its worsening relations with almost all Western countries, including the United States, and with pro-Western countries in its proximity isolated Iran in many other parts of the globe. In its severe form, its isolation continued until 1997 when Iranian President Mohammad Khatami launched a policy of easing tension with regional and non-regional countries. Its implementation significantly improved Iranian relations with the EU, Persian Gulf, and Middle Eastern countries.

Despite its peaceful ties with those countries, Iran is still highly isolated internationally. In particular, this undesirable situation is reflected in three major ways with an important political and economic impact on the country. First, while the Iran-Iraq War ended in 1988, Iran's failure to achieve the full implementation of the UNSC resolutions of 1988 and 1990 regarding its ceasefire with Iraq is a clear sign of its international isolation. This situation made it unable to receive its internationally recognized rights from the highly isolated Iraqi regime which collapsed in April 2003. It has yet to resolve its disputes with Iraq on many issues such as the return of the Iranian POWs and to receive $100 billion in reparation as stipulated by a UNSC resolution. Given Iraq's occupation by the American military, any success in these areas will be pending the normalization of Iranian-American relations or at least a thaw in those relations. Second, the imposition of a variety of American economic sanctions on Iran observed by just about all the countries with normal relations with Iran, including the European countries, is yet another indicator of its isolation. Among other negative impacts, the latter has created barriers to Iran's acquisition of advanced technology and products not just from the United States, but also from many other countries. As a recent example, in September 2002 the European consortium producing Airbus civilian airplanes had to cancel its contract with Iran for the purchase of hundreds of millions of dollars worth of airplanes, although Iran had already paid for them.[54] The fact that they contained American engines made certain American sanctions applicable to those European aircraft. Airbus Corporation now has to find European substitutes for those engines in order to reactive its contract with Iran, a difficult task given the widespread use of American parts in European aircraft industry. Finally, Iran's isolation has been reflected in its failure to settle the division of the Caspian Sea with other littoral states through a multilateral agreement. The result has been the conclusion of bilateral agreements between Russian and Kazakhstan in May 2002 and between Russia and Azerbaijan in September 2002. Those agreements have undermined Iran's role in finding a legal regime for the Caspian Sea in a manner to preserve its national interests, while leaving it in a very difficult negotiating position with the other four Caspian littoral states.

In a sense, though different from that of Iran, Russia is also isolated. The fall of the Soviet Union was initially thought to end its successive state's isolation, the type experienced by the Soviet Union, which confined it to have extensive ties mainly with its ideological bloc members. The Russians hoped that the end of the Cold War would open to them the doors of the Western countries. Theoretically, that would make them a fully-integrated country in the world economy and would qualify them to enjoy high political influence in world affairs. Needless to say, Russia has normalized its relations with its ex-foes, namely the Western countries. Although it no longer has Cold War hostile relations with them, it has failed to achieve its hoped-for objectives. Its friendly ties with those countries have not paralleled significant economic relations. In the post–Cold War era, thanks to its weak and declining economy and its eroding military strength, Russia has become a marginalized state in the international system with little influence, if anything at all, in major international affairs such as the Arab-Israeli conflict and the political developments in the Balkans. This is despite its UNSC permanent membership, which, during the Cold War was a guarantee for its exercising influence in world affairs.

Despite its preeminent nuclear capability and its UNSC permanent membership, certain factors have paved the way for Russia's practical isolation in the international arena. One major factor has been its declining global influence caused by its numerous domestic problems. Other important factors have included the loss of its former bloc of states, friends, and allies, its inability to form a new alliance, and its failure to even keep together the CIS countries all of which are now following their own national interests. Finally, its severe economic problems and its diminishing military might have formed two other majoʳ contributing factors to Russia's isolation. In short, the sudden loss of Russia's might and its practical demotion to the rank of a second-rate state at the time when Western political, economic, and military blocs are growing around it created a sense of isolation and marginalization for the Russians. Given its insignificant economic capability compared to its large population as reflected in its small GDP ($401 billion in 1999),[55] the recent mainly ceremonial membership of Russia in G-8 summits has not changed this sentiment radically.

For certain reasons, India also feels isolated, although it has peaceful ties with a wide range of countries. This is a result of its inability to achieve its desired eminent international status, despite India's certain qualifications, including its large area, its large population, and its nuclear capability. The Indians feel that the international system systematically discriminates against them the way they were treated in the long period of British colonization. In particular, India's failure to turn its nuclear status into a winning card to elevate its international status as it hoped for has reinforced its sense of alienation with the international system. This failure has contributed to the Indians' sense of isolation in world affairs.[56]

Despite having different backgrounds, a different pattern of relationship with foreign countries, and different overall capabilities, Iran, India, and Russia share a sense of isolation in world affairs. This has created an additional ground for a natural trend toward cooperation among them backed by certain facilitating parameters. Of these, the most important ones are their historical ties, common, close, or similar views on certain regional and international issues, and the realities of their current unsatisfactory situation with all its restrictions.

IMPACT OF ECONOMIC FACTORS ON THE POLARIZATION PROCESS

The push for cooperation and close ties between and among Iran, India, and Russia has not stemmed only from political and security realities. The three countries also have strong economic incentives to work closely with each other. Close economic contacts between India and Russia began almost right after India's independence. Coming out of a few centuries of British colonization, the Indians, who had a very negative view about the Western countries and who were very sensitive about their independence, found ties with the Soviet Union plausible. For its part, the latter was also interested in such relations as it was in search of new friends, allies, and markets outside its newly formed eastern European bloc. Moreover, along with Yugoslavia, India's leadership of the nonaligned movement also inclined New Delhi to forge extensive economic relations with Russia's predecessor, the Soviet Union. The movement encouraged a third bloc of countries independent from the two rival superpowers and their allies, while maintaining relations with their blocs. Added to that, India's weak financial capability made the significantly less expensive Soviet products more affordable than Western ones. Finally, along with its bloc members, the Soviet Union became the main available industrialized state willing to help India achieve its main objective of consolidating its independence and preparing a basis for its rise as a great power. That required a strong industrial sector, a strong military force backed by an indigenous military industry, a large scientific core, and a modern and extensive infrastructure. India lacked all of these conditions at the time of independence. Thus, the Soviet Union, and to a lesser extent its bloc members, became the main source of transfer of technology and advanced equipment for India. They helped the Indians create a strong industrial sector, including a heavy industry consisting of a large military branch producing many Soviet-designed weapons under licence, while enabling it to embark on a variety of scientific projects. As well, the Soviets helped the Indians form a military force through their transfer to India of technology, know-how, and training, and by selling advanced weapons to it. Therefore the Soviets became the main arms supplier to India. In short, mutual interests helped India and the Soviet Union forge economic and military relations, which grew on a steady basis until the Soviet Union's fall.

This pattern of cooperation has continued in the post–Soviet era. This is partly because of their friendly relations based on historical reasons and on their close views concerning major regional and international issues. It is also partly because of strict economic realities such as India's financial difficulties, which make inexpensive Russian products tempting. Other realities include the heavy dependency of India's industries and military on Russian parts and equipment, and India's lack of internationally marketable products with a few exceptions (e.g., computer software). For its part, Russia's inability to find new markets has inclined it to continue its ties with India. This is in addition to its long-term thinking, as having access to the growing Indian market is of strategic importance for Russia. In 2002, the Russian government's licensing India for the production of 140 Sokhoi 30 fighter aircraft serves as a recent example of the Indian market's importance for the Russian economy.[57]

As well, Iran and Russia have become close to each other for economic reasons. As mentioned earlier, since the last years of the Soviet Union, Moscow and Tehran have had expanding multidimensional economic ties. The same reasons justifying Russia's economic relations with India have also motivated its economic ties with Iran. In this regard, the main difference has been Iran's much stronger financial capability as a major oil-exporting country, which has made the Iranian market a very promising one for the Russians. Their high hopes for increasing their share of that market were reflected in the Russian government's revealing of a proposed plan in 2002 on expanding Iranian-Russian annual trade to $5 billion and on Russia's sale of $3 billion worth of advanced weapons, including aircraft, submarines, and air defence systems.[58] As well, the Russians announced their readiness to sell six more nuclear power reactors to Iran.[59]

Apart from bilateral economic relations, Iran, India, and Russia have found common grounds for forging trilateral economic relations. Their cordial and friendly ties as well as their geographical locations have put them in a position to embark on certain major projects. If fully implemented, those projects have the potential to boost their economies and uplift their international status. Recently, there have been two major trilateral projects. One is the North-South Corridor agreement as discussed earlier. Another is a major gas pipeline project.

On 12 November 2002, Russia's Gazprom announced its plan to construct an undersea gas pipeline between Iran and India for exporting Iranian natural gas to India via Pakistan.[60] According to the announcement, the Russian company has reached an agreement in principle with Iran for the project.[61] By signing a note of understanding, it has also received Pakistan's consent for the passage of the pipeline through its territorial waters.[62] In addition to transit fees, the Pakistanis will receive gas from the pipeline. If the pipeline's construction actually begins, the $3.2 billion pipeline project will be a major political and economic achievement for Iran, India, and Russia.

The idea of exporting Iranian gas to Pakistan and to India via Pakistan emerged in the 1990s. Toward the end of those years, a significant number of large and small companies expressed their readiness to take part in such a project. For example, in 1998, the Iranian Mostazafan va Jonbazan Foundation announced its plan to form a joint venture with Shell, British Gas, and Petronass to lay a 1,400-kilometer gas pipeline between Iran's Persian Gulf South Pars gas field to Karachi in Pakistan.[63] Also, Royal Dutch Shell expressed an interest in a pipeline project to connect this offshore Iranian gas field to Moritan in India.[64] As well, Australia became enthusiastic to join a trilateral project with Iran and India to export Iranian gas to India.[65] In particular, one of its energy companies (BHP), which expressed its interest in laying a gas pipeline connecting the South Pars gas field to Pakistan and India, even conducted a technical and economic assessment on the proposed project.[66] However, none of the mentioned expressions of interest turned into a contract for the actual construction of a pipeline. For this matter, Gazprom's announcement is of significance as, for the first time, a major gas company has actually gone beyond the expression of interest. It is also important as Gazprom is one of the three companies developing Iran's South Pars gas field, along with French Total and Malaysian Petronass. India will receive Iranian gas from this gas field.

Moreover the announcement is important for its including the Pakistani consent without which the construction of the shortest possible pipeline to India will be simply impossible. As envisaged, the pipeline will be laid at the depth of 150 meters within Pakistan's Arabian Sea territorial waters to reach India through the neighboring Indian Ocean. For its domestic consumption, Pakistan will receive gas through a branch pipeline connecting the main pipeline to Pakistan. Despite its major conflicts with India, three factors seem to have convinced the Pakistanis to give their consent for the project. First, it will address their need for imported gas from the closest and the most reliable exporter, that is their neighboring Iran. Despite their conflict of interests in Afghanistan over the last two decades, many political, economic, and security considerations have encouraged Iran and Pakistan to maintain peaceful relations. While details of the arrangements are yet to be released, it is safe to assume that Iran should have offered a reasonable price for its gas to be sold to Pakistan to make the Pakistanis interested in the project. Second, the lucrative nature of the pipeline project should have sweetened the deal for the Pakistanis. They will receive an unspecified amount of transit fees for the passage of gas through their territorial waters. Given Pakistan's limited financial means and its growing financial needs, an expected significant amount of annual revenue in transit fees will be of importance to the Pakistani economy. Third, a gas pipeline to India via Pakistan could help reduce tension and the threat of war between the two neighbors through creating stakes not just for Pakistan, but also for India in peaceful relations between the two countries. Aside from their current propaganda war, neither side wants nor can afford a full-scale war with a possibility of escalation into a nuclear exchange. However, the removal of such a possibility requires a reduction of tension in their relations.

Gazprom's announcement was definitely a significant step toward the construction of the gas pipeline to India, but it is still too early to be certain about the full implementation of the Iranian-Russian-Pakistani agreement. According to the Russian company, it will send a delegation to Iran in 2003 to prepare grounds for the creation of a working team to study the technical and economic aspects of the pipeline project. However, neither that company nor Iran has yet specified a date for the actual beginning of its construction. As a result, it is not yet clear when and if the project will become a reality in the near future. Nevertheless, if implemented, the Iranian-Pakistani-Indian pipeline project will be a significant development both for its economic importance and political implications. As a large and growing Asian market, India will be a major importer of fossil energy, including natural gas, in the twenty-first century. Iran's securing access to that market will end its current insignificant gas exports to turn it into a major global gas exporter. The latter will provide the Iranians with long-term large annual revenues, a necessity for financing their numerous unfinished projects estimated at about 45,000 and for diversifying their oil-dependent economy, among addressing other problems. The deal also will be a major success for Russia whose oil and gas companies have sought to turn themselves into major international players. As Iran has the world's second largest gas deposit, Russia's involvement in its export project will certainly grant the Russians who possess the world's largest gas reserves a very strong position in the international gas markets.

If the envisaged gas pipeline is constructed, it will be another step toward closer cooperation among the three dissatisfied regional powers, India, Iran, and Russia, without regard to the American D'Amato Act. The latter bans any foreign investment in the Iranian energy industry over the American-set limit of $20 million. In particular, such a development will be a setback for American foreign policy toward Iran, which seeks Iran's economic weakness and international isolation, while being yet another source of conflict in Russian-American relations.

China's Ties with Iran, India, and Russia

China has also found a strong incentive to seek close ties with Iran and Russia individually, while remaining unenthusiastic about extensive ties with India. Chinese-Indian relations are peaceful, but not warm and growing because of historical reasons, including their 1962 war and Indian-Soviet and Chinese-Pakistani close ties. Another major reason is the Chinese and the Indian bid to establish themselves as global powers with a strong role in Asian affairs, which makes them rivals in Asia. As for China's ties with Russia, the Chinese may not be a long-term ally of the Russians as they pursue the objective of turning themselves into a global nuclear power. This puts them on a course of rivalry with Russia seeking to regain its pre-eminent international status as a superpower. Having said that, China's ties with Russia have been peaceful and friendly for over a decade. In particular, their economic and military relations have been growing. In 2001, the value of the Chinese-Russian trade was about $8 billion.[67] This is a result of Russia's limited success in finding markets elsewhere for its exportable products and of China's need to address its deficiencies in certain areas difficult to be addressed through other advanced economies for political and economic reasons. As mentioned earlier, military sales have accounted for the major part of their trade. This fact makes Russia the main supplier of advanced arms to China in search of such arms to modernize its conventional forces.

Iran and China have been on friendly terms for over three decades since the Shah regime established relations with China in the early 1970s. The 1979 revolution turned China into a major friend of Iran and gradually a major economic partner, thanks to Iran's isolation and the imposition of trade sanctions on Iran by just about all its major and large trade partners (i.e., the Western economies). Added to that, Iran's military needs during the Iran-Iraq War forced it to resort to China as a main supplier of arms. This became a necessity, given Iran's loss of its pre-1979 arms supplier (i.e., the Western countries, particularly the United States, and the Soviet Union). Surprisingly enough, the Soviets supplied about 15 percent of Iran's military needs, including amphibious armoured vehicles and heavy artillery pieces. Facing a worldwide sanction on arms sales to Iran and the Soviet Union's taking sides with Iraq, Iran had to expand ties with two willing arms suppliers, namely China and North Korea. In the post-war era beginning in 1988, friendly relations based on sharing similar or close views on major regional and international issues have reinforced their interests in continuing extensive economic relations justified by economic imperatives on both sides. Those justifications include the existence of a variety of sanctions on Iran, the attractiveness of inexpensive Chinese products for financially squeezed Iran, and China's need for imported oil and inexpensive Iranian consumer products. These relations have actually extended as Iran has embarked on many developmental and reconstruction programs in this period. Among other activities, China has become involved in meeting some of Iran's needs in heavy industry, including the construction of large power generators. In 2002, the Iranian-Chinese trade was valued at about $2 billion.

FACTORS CONTRIBUTING TO AN AMERICAN-PAKISTANI ALLIANCE

While there are certain reasons for the creation of a grouping among Iran, India, and Russia, certain factors also help the formation of an alliance between the United States and Pakistan. Although their alliance will unlikely last for a long time, following the pattern of their relations in the 1980s and the 1990s, the two countries have certain common interests that lay the foundation for the alliance.

First, the interests of Pakistan and the United States in Afghanistan and Central Asia coincide. Pakistan has a strong interest in controlling its neighboring Afghanistan, both for its own merits and also for its providing access to Central Asia where the Pakistanis have stakes. The latter corresponds to the Americans' interest in having a stable and pro-American Afghanistan as a springboard for them in South and West Asia and also as a bridge to access Central Asia without passing through Iran and Russia. In particular, a stable Afghanistan will make the Pakistani route to export Caspian oil and gas a feasible option for the Americans who have been in search of reliable long-term routes for such an export. While arising from two different strategic objectives, the compatibility of the Pakistani and American interests in Afghanistan and Central Asia has formed the foundation for their alliance. After a decade of uneasy relations worsened by Pakistan's nuclear tests in 1998, the American war in Afghanistan necessitated Pakistan's cooperation. This necessity paved the way for an alliance between the two countries.

Second, the American and Pakistani hostility to or concern about certain countries has also provided grounds for their alliance. They have common concerns about Iran, which they want to "contain" for different long-term reasons. As mentioned before, they are both concerned about its rise as a regional power capable of challenging other regional and nonregional states with a stake in the regions in its proximity. The existing American-Iranian hostile ties have made Iran's industrialization, its expanding military capabilities, and its growing influence in certain strategic regions (i.e., the Persian Gulf, the Middle East, the Caucasus, and Central Asia) a worrisome trend for the Americans. Unlike the Americans, the Pakistanis have peaceful relations and economic ties with their neighboring Iran. However, they are concerned about Iran for its position as a rival regional power. While Iran has sought to make itself the main, or at least a main, transit route for the international trade of the Central Asians and the Caucasians, including their oil and gas exports, Pakistan has also sought to establish itself as a route. Now that objective has the backing of the Americans who view Pakistan as an ally.

Iran's extensive ties with India are also a source of concern for Pakistan, although they have not yet grown into an anti-Pakistani military alliance. However, the common interest of Iran and India in keeping Pakistan in check and preventing its penetration into Central Asia creates grounds for concern in Pakistan. The fragile nature of peace between India and Pakistan makes a military confrontation between the two countries a realistic scenario with a predictable undesirable outcome for Pakistan, since the Indians are strong enough to inflict another defeat on the Pakistanis. As mentioned before, this fragility has been reflected in tension along the Indian-Pakistani border in Kashmir. The two countries' show of force in the form of missile tests has revealed the dangerous nature of the threat. As a recent example, in October 2002 Pakistan test-fired a medium-range missile called *Shaheen* to provoke an Indian test fire of an anti-missile missile called *Akash*.[68] Against this background, the situation could become even worse should Iran join India in an anti-Pakistani alliance. In such a case, Pakistan would be sandwiched between two hostile states bordering it in the west and in the east.

Regarding India, Pakistan and the United States do not see eye to eye. Whereas it is a clear source of threat for the former, the latter considers it a potential long-term source of threat under certain circumstances. The United States is not on hostile terms with India and sees it, as it also did in the 1960s and the 1970s, as a regional power potentially capable of keeping China in check to some extent. Moreover, the Americans are interested in the large Indian market, which, in the absence of its current barriers to foreign products and investments, could be lucrative owing to the enlargement of the Indian middle class. Yet, their regional interests demand working with Pakistan at least in the short run. Whether the Americans like it or not, that fact makes extensive ties with India rather difficult, if not impossible, notwithstanding India's interest in the American market for its computer software exports. Given the depth of hostility between India and Pakistan, the Americans' siding with the Pakistanis for their regional interests put them in an unwanted hostile situation with India. The scope and objectives of U.S. relations with Pakistan and the type of assistance the Americans provide to the Pakistanis will determine the extent of the Indians' hostility toward the Americans. As for the Americans, India's missile and nuclear capability which is more advanced than Pakistan's is not posing a military threat for the time being. However, it will be a source of concern should India and Russia close ranks while American-Russian relations deteriorate.

With respect to China, Pakistan and the United States are on opposite sides. For Pakistan, China has been a great friend for over four decades. For different reasons, their mutually shared dissatisfaction with the Americans has brought them close to each other. As well, their common mistrust and hostility toward India has cemented not just their economic and political ties, but also their military and nuclear cooperation. As a matter of fact, to a great extent, Pakistan owes its advancement in missile development and, to a lesser extent, in nuclear weapon production to China, which has transferred to Pakistan certain technology, equipment, and expertise.[69] Arising from their hostility toward both China and Pakistan, the Indians attribute all Pakistan's military advancement, including its nuclear and missile projects, to China's full transfer of all the requirements as they did in October 2002 after Pakistan's test-firing of the medium-range missile *Shaheen*. In her reaction to the test, Indian foreign ministry spokeswoman Nirupama Rao stated: "As we have said before, we are not particularly impressed with these missile antics of Pakistan. It is well known that Pakistan's missiles are based on clandestinely imported material, equipment and technology."[70] Although she did not name China, it was quite clear that she was referring to that country as the Indians always do. To remove any doubt about India's view on this matter, Indian Defense Minister George Fernandes spelled it out in the same month during his speech at a convention of the ruling Bharatiya Janata Party (BJP) in Mumbai when he said: "Everyone knows what Pakistan will be without China. Its ego is boosted purely by the support it gets from China."[71] Although this is an understandably exaggerated statement, it demonstrates to a great extent China's importance for Pakistan's military development. Consequently, the American interest in containing China does not coincide with the long-term interests of Pakistan seeing China as its strategic friend—a friend, which, unlike the United States, as the Pakistanis believe, stood by Pakistan in 1965 and 1971 when it was at war with India.[72]

For the United States, containing China and Russia is a major objective behind its deploying forces in South and West Asia. Respectively, as a rising nuclear and re-rising superpower, the Americans are looking at their alliance with Pakistan as a means to that end. When it comes to Russia, the Pakistanis do not have the same long-term thinking of the Americans, but they agree with their objective because of their own hostility toward India. This makes sense from the standpoint of weakening India's main ally and its main arms supplier, a major factor in India's military superiority. However, due to the importance of China as their strategic ally, the Pakistanis cannot support the American objective of containing China.

Depending on regional and international developments, the Americans may change their pattern of regional alliance, including that with Pakistan, but Pakistan does not have that option. This is a function of its much weaker economic and military power and its limited regional and international political influence. Added to this, the Pakistanis negative past experience with the United States has made them reluctant to damage their relations with China, a regional power with a nuclear capability far larger than that of India and in need of an ally like Pakistan for a long time. In particular, the American record of letting the Pakistanis down, as they describe the American behavior during their 1965 and 1971 wars with India, makes the Pakistanis suspicious of the long-term reliability of their new ally, while creating a strong disincentive for alienating China. The Pakistanis have long blamed the Americans for refusing to change the tide of war in Pakistan's favor in the mentioned wars with India when it was facing the much stronger enemy.[73] Despite Pakistan's status as the American ally in the Indian Ocean facing India, a Soviet ally, their refusal to use their diplomatic influence and to provide the Pakistanis with advanced weapons contributed to the latter's loss of the two wars. In addition to the bitterness of any military defeat, the loss of then East Pakistan to become Bangladesh in the aftermath of the 1971 Indian-Pakistani war has since left a deep sense of mistrust toward the United States among the Pakistanis. In both wars, China stood behind Pakistan and supplied it with Chinese arms, although they were no match for the state-of-the-art Soviet weapons used by the Indians.[74] Apart from this bitter memory, the Pakistanis' negative experience in their ties with the Americans include the latter's imposition of economic and military sanctions on Pakistan in the 1980s and 1990s. As a result, they cancelled the sale to Pakistan of the badly needed F-16 fighters as a punishment for its nuclear program.

NOTES

1. RFE/RL, 24 August 2002.
2. Ibid.
3. James Brooke, "Putin Greets North Korean Leader on Russia's Pacific Coast," *The New York Times,* 24 August 2002.

4. Ibid.

5. "Guard Tries to Kill President," *Guardian* (unlimited), 5 September 2002.

6. "Iranian President Condemns Assassination Attempt on President Karzai," *Ettela'at Binolmelali* (Tehran), 9 August 2002, 2.

7. Mohammad Naseen Shafaq and Habiburahman Ibrahimi, ISAF Promises Crackdown on Saboteurs, Institute of War and Peace Reporting, 20 January 2003.

8. "Guard Tries to Kill President," *Guardian* (unlimited), 5 September 2002.

9. "The World This Week," *The Economist,* 31 August 2002, 6; The Global Development Briefing (hereafter GDB), 26 September 2002; News, Radio of the Islamic Republic of Iran, 14 October 2002.

10. Drug Abuse Prevention, Republic of Belarus, info@nodrug.by, www.correspondent.net, 28 July, 2001.

11. For an account on the reasons for India to develop a military nuclear capability, see: Hooman Peimani, *Nuclear Proliferation in the Indian Subcontinent: The Self-Exhausting "Superpowers" and Emerging Alliances* (Westport, CT: Praeger, 2000), 21–26.

12. For details on the Turkmenchai Treaty, see: Bahram Amirahmadian, "The Trend of Developments in the Karabakh Crisis," *Majelieh-e Motaellat-e Asyaie Markazi va Ghafghaz* [Central Asia and the Caucasus Review] (Tehran), 28 (Winter 2000), 32.

13. Iran has created a strong industrial basis, which, despite its shortcomings, enables it to embark on major developmental projects. For details see: Hooman Peimani, *Iran and the United States: The Rise of the West Asian Regional Grouping* (Westport, CT: Praeger, 1999), 49–59.

14. Thomas Woodrow, "China Rising, America Sleeping," The Jamestown Foundation, 1 August 2002, republished by Information, info@mail.uyghurinfo.com, Central Asia News, 2 August 2002, 12:03:55-0700 (PDT). (Internet publication)

15. The World Bank. *World Development Indicators 2001* (Washington, D.C.: The World Bank, 2001), 208.

16. Drug Abuse Prevention.

17. Text: President Putin's State of the Nation Address, Unofficial translation of full text by Vladimir Vladimirovich Putin, The Russian Observer, Observer.com. Issued on 04.18.2002 (MST).

18. Steven Lee Meyers, "Russia Recasts Bog in Caucasus as War on Terror," *The New York Times,* 2 October 2002. (Internet version)

19. Hooman Peimani, *Failed Transition, Bleak Future? War and Instability in Central Asia and the Caucasus* (Westport, CT: Praeger, 2002), 82–83.

20. UNDP, *Human Development Report 2001* (New York: Oxford University Press, 2001), 154–155, 191.

21. "Nato Strikes Deal to Accept Russia in a Partnership," *The New York Times,* 15 May 2002. (Internet version)

22. Ibid.

23. News. BBC World, 14 November 2002.

24. "Opinion Poll Results Indicate Dissatisfaction," *Ettela'at Binolmelali* (Tehran), 21 October 2002, 4.

25. "Released Opinion Poll Results Provoke Harsh Reactions," *Ettela'at Binolmelali* (Tehran), 24 October 2002, 4.

26. RFE/RL, 27 October 2002.

27. REF/RL, 2 November 2002.

28. See Amnesty International reports in September 2002.

29. "Student Protests Held at Tehran Campuses," *Abrar* (Tehran), 18 November 2002, 2.

30. Hooman Peimani, "The Ties That Bind Iran and Saudi Arabia," *Asia Time online* (Hong Kong), 16 August 2002; Hooman Peimani, "Bahrain Turns to Iran," *Asia Time online* (Hong Kong), 22 August 2002; Hooman Peimani, "Iran and Kuwait Close Ranks," *Asia Time online* (Hong Kong), 25 September 2002.

31. Peimani, "The Ties That Bind Iran and Saudi Arabia."

32. For a detailed analysis of various shortcomings of the Baku-Tiblisi-Ceyhan pipeline, see: Hooman Peimani, *The Caspian Pipeline Dilemma: Political Games and Economic Losses* (Westport, CT: Praeger, 2001), 77–108.

33. "Kazakhstan and Russia Sign Agreement on Oil Transit," volume 7, issue #13—Thursday, 27 June, 2002. (Internet version)

34. Ibid.

35. Ibid.

36. "Turkey," Eia Country Analysis Brief, July 2002 (eia-doe.gov).

37. REF/RL, 7 October 2002.

38. "Zangene: We Resolved Our Export Problem," *Hamsahrye* (Tehran), 10 October 2002, 2.

39. Hooman Peimani, "Caspian Sea Divide No Closer to Closure," *Asia Times online* (Hong Kong), 19 April 2002.

40. Ibid.

41. Ibid.

42. Michael Lelyveld, "Caspian: U.S. Says Patrol Boats Are Gifts to Promote Regional Security," REF/RL, 26 June 2001.

43. Ibid.

44. Hooman Peimani, *Regional Security and the Future of Central Asia: The Competition of Iran, Turkey, and Russia* (Westport, CT: Praeger, 1998), 83.

45. For an account on the factors contributing to the creation of the Kashmiri conflict and the first Indian-Pakistani war, see: Maj. Gen. Sukhwant Singh, *India's War Since Independence* (New Delhi: Lancer, 1986); Karim Saddiqui, *Conflicts, Crisis, and War in Pakistan* (Lahore: Macmillan, 1974).

46. For details on the Indian and Pakistani nuclear strength, see: Peimani, *Nuclear Proliferation in the Indian Subcontinent*, 53.

47. Ziba Moshaver, *Nuclear Weapons Proliferation in the Indian Subcontinent* (New York: St. Martin's Press, 1991), 36.

48. Elisabeth Rosenthal, "China Seems to Deny Pakistan a Nuclear Umbrella," *The New York Times*, 21 May 1998. (Internet version)

49. Erik Eckholm, "American Gives Beijing Good News: Rebels on Terror List," *The New York Times*, 26 August 2002. (Internet version)

50. "U.S. Concern: Moscow-Beijing Arms Deals," UPI, 30 November 2000, accessed via NewsMax.com Wires.

51. UNDP, *Human Development Report 2001* (New York: Oxford University Press, 2001), 179–180.

52. Ibid.

53. 2001 National Trade Estimate Report on Foreign Trade Barriers, United States Department of Trade, website.

54. "Airbus Sale Fell Through," 1 October 2002, *Iran* (Tehran), 1.

55. UNDP. *Human Development Report 2001* (New York: Oxford University Press, 2001), 179.

56. For detailed information on India's objectives behind its achievement of a nuclear status and factors contributing to its disappointment since 1998, see: Hooman Peimani, *Nuclear Proliferation in the Indian Subcontinent: The Self-Exhausting "Superpowers" and Emerging Alliances* (Westport, CT: Praeger, 2000), 21–26.

57. Jamestown Foundation, *Monitor,* Vol 8 (76), 18 April 2002.

58. "Military Buildup Ends US-Russian Honeymoon," *Asia Times online* (Hong Kong), 29 August 2002.

59. Ibid.

60. REF/RL, 12 November 2002.

61. Ibid.

62. Ibid.

63. "MJF Plans to Invest $3 Billion in Gas Pipeline to Pakistan," *Ettela'at Binolmelali* (Tehran), 5 February 1998, 12.

64. "An American Expert: The USA Has No Choice but to Remove Sanction Against Iran," *Ettela'at Binolmelali* (Tehran), 30 April 1998, 1.

65. "Australia Voices Readiness to Invest in Iran Oil Projects," *Ettela'at Binolmelali* (Tehran), 26 May 1998, 12.

66. "Project for the Transfer of Gas of the South Pars Field to India and Pakistan Will Begin," *Abrar* (Tehran), 9 April 1998, 4.

67. "Russia, China Sign Friendship Treaty," Associated Press, 16 July 2001.

68. Ranjit Devraj, "China Behind Pakistan's Missile Tests, Says India," *Asia Time online,* 8 October 2002.

69. For a detailed account on China's involvement in Pakistan's nuclear weapon and missile development, see: Peimani, *Nuclear Proliferation in the Indian Subcontinent,* 12–18, 20–21.

70. Devraj.

71. Ibid.

72. For a Pakistani view on the role of the United States and China during their 1965 and 1971 wars, see: S. Saliq, *Witness to Surrender* (Karachi: Oxford University Press, 1978); see also: Karim Saddiqui, *Conflict, Crisis, and War in Pakistan* (Lahore: Macmillan, 1972).

73. Moshaver, 20.

74. Peimani, *Nuclear Proliferation in the Indian Subcontinent,* 107–109; see also, A. H. Rizvi, *The Military and Politics in Pakistan* (Lahore: Progressive Publishers, 1974).

5

Conclusion

Certain events following the September 11 terrorist attacks on the United States have had a major impact on the political structure of South and West Asia. The American war on terrorist groups in Afghanistan facilitated the Taliban regime's fall and ended the long Afghan civil war to open a new era for war-torn Afghanistan. The fall and the subsequent formation of an Afghan interim government created hope for stability and peace for the country devastated by over two decades of war in different forms. Despite the interest of the Afghans and their neighbors for a stable, peaceful, and predictable Afghanistan, the post–Taliban era has failed to meet the expectations. Apart from a few positive changes such as a relatively improved status for women, post–Taliban Afghanistan has all the symptoms of instability with a strong potential for developing into a new round of civil war. The reemergence of warlords all over the country, the expansion of turf war among them, the expanding lawlessness, and the weakness of the central government to establish its authority beyond the presidential palace in Kabul make that undesirable scenario feasible in the near future.

The American war on terrorism in Afghanistan has suddenly expanded the political and military presence of the United States in West and South Asia. In addition to Afghanistan, its military forces have been deployed or reinforced in Kyrgyzstan, Uzbekistan, Georgia, and in almost all the Arab Persian Gulf countries. About two years after the deployment of the first American units in Afghanistan, it is now quite clear that the American military presence in those countries will last much longer than required by the need to conduct the American war against the remnants of the Taliban and al-Qaeda in Afghanistan. In itself, the end of that war seems to be anybody's guess, given an increase in the small-scale, hit-and-run operations of those groups against the Afghan and American forces in late 2002, which continued in the first half of 2003. The anti-Taliban/al-Qaeda war seems to be far from over after about two years of military operations. Apart from the impact on the American troop deployment of a prolonged military operation in Afghanistan, certain strategic interests have convinced the American government to keep its troops all over South and West Asia for an indefinite period of time.

The American anti-terrorist war has changed the political and security structure of South and West Asia. Many regional countries joined the Americans in that war right after 11 September 2001 when the legitimate objective of fighting Afghanistan-based terrorist groups, a menace to a variety of regional and nonregional countries, created a common ground for their cooperation, in one form or another. However, that "grand" anti-terrorist alliance could not last very long. The development was the "natural" result of the "evolution" of war on terrorism as an objective into other objectives on both sides of the equation. This was due to the vague nature of the initial objective around which the so-called regional alliance was created. While all the regional countries, like just about all other countries, committed themselves to cooperation to uproot terrorism and in particular the Afghanistan-based terrorists, the regional alliance, in its explicit and implicit forms, began to erode a few months after its formation in late 2001. The main reason was the absence of a strong common denominator to keep all its contributing members together. "Fighting terrorism" was not a clear objective to become a uniting factor for the countries as any "alliance" member had its own self-serving understanding of that objective. In fact, under the banner of fighting terrorism, each has since sought to achieve its own national interests, mainly unrelated to the announced objectives. China, Russia, and the Central Asian countries (Uzbekistan, Kyrgyzstan, and Kazakhstan) have taken the "golden" opportunity to deal with their internal opposition groups of different nature, peaceful and violent alike. Similarly, the United States has sought to consolidate its influence in certain regions of strategic importance to its national interests, namely the Persian Gulf, the Caucasus and Central Asia.

Unsurprisingly, the alliance has been disintegrating, in the absence of a common objective for long-term collaboration. In such a situation, the "war on terrorism" itself has functioned as a catalyst to provoke a political division in South and West Asia by helping polarize them into two groupings or camps of rival states with long-term interests in those regions. Future developments will determine whether those camps can take implicit or explicit forms. In particular, concerns about the political, economic, and military expansion of the United States in the two neighboring regions and those of Pakistan with the latter's backing have created a concern strong enough to facilitate the polarization process. On the one side, there are Iran, India, and Russia. Based on their well-established bilateral ties and their common, close, or similar views on major regional and international issues, they have become closer to each other since the early 1990s. Their political closeness and the compatibility of their major interests will likely lead to their forming an implicit or explicit alliance, if the current pattern of threat and friendship continues. Regardless of its form, such an alliance will aim at helping them deal with the rising threat of political, economic, and military nature posed by the United States and its regional ally, Pakistan.

Sharing their concerns and views on a variety of issues such as the expanding American presence in its neighboring regions, China is an affiliated member of the emerging "camp." Despite its current friendly and extensive relations with Iran and Russia and its peaceful relations with India, certain factors will prevent it from committing itself to any alliance forged by the two states and Iran. These are its historically uneasy ties with India and Russia and its rivalry with the latter as a rising nuclear power. Until it can find an alternative market, China's extensive trade with the United States will create yet another disincentive for the Chinese to join that camp as a full member. Likewise, its well-established, extensive relations with Pakistan and the importance of that country for China both for its own merits and also for its utility in China's dealing with India will weaken further its incentive to take sides with Iran, India, and Russia as a group. However, having various reasons for grievances with the United States, one should expect its taking sides with the camp or its members individually on specific issues of common interest, such as regional security.

On the other side, a Pakistani-American camp exists. Unlike the mentioned emerging camp, this one is an explicit alliance based on certain common interests. Those interests include an Afghanistan run by a docile and friendly government for security considerations and for their need of that country as a springboard to project their power in its neighboring regions. Also, they include their interest in having access to the landlocked Central Asian countries where both wish to expand politically and economically. As well, they include their interest in blocking the regional advancement of certain states, mainly Iran and Russia, while each has an additional interest in containing India, in the case of Pakistan, and keeping in check China, in the case of the United States. Finally, for the Pakistanis, aligning with the United States in its war on terrorism has helped them address some of their economic problems, particularly their severe financial difficulties. Thus, they have managed to reschedule their debt payments and to receive financial aid packages.

In spite of its benefits for both sides, the American-Pakistani alliance will not likely last for a long time. On both sides, there are diverging interests provoking "defection" in the future. For Pakistan, the U.S. objective of containing China is unacceptable, owing to its long history of relations with its neighboring China. For its immediate and strategic reasons, China has assisted Pakistan since the 1960s, including during its wars with India. The Chinese have helped the Pakistanis with their industrialization projects and scientific research in military and non-military fields, including their nuclear and missile projects. Given their shared concern about India, China and Pakistan have a strong stake in continuing their collaboration and friendship. In particular, the Pakistanis do not see America as a reliable long-term ally given its refusal to help them when the Pakistanis needed it most (i.e., during their 1965 and 1971 wars with India). America's unreliability in those occasions stemmed from its interest in having a strong India to help it contain China. Although the hostile pattern of Sino-American relations is long disappeared, the American concern about the rising China will probably justify sacrificing Pakistan to please India should the need arise. This possibility aside, changing regional alliances is necessary and feasible for a superpower like the United States, because of its extensive presence and various interest all over the planet as well as its gigantic economic resources. The latter enables it to tolerate large losses caused by a sudden shift of alliance for the sake of its strategic interests. A regional power like Pakistan with very limited available resources does not have this type of luxury. In particular, because of the strategic significance of its ties with China, it is highly unlikely for Pakistan to join America in its containment of China.

For the United States, Pakistan is an important ally because of its need for that country to help it achieve some of its strategic objectives in South and West Asia. However, in the long run, India will be a more interesting ally given its "traditional" suspicion and animosity toward China and, compared to Pakistan, its far stronger scientific, economic, and military capability, conventional and nuclear alike. Although there is no strong evidence to suggest that the Indians may be interested in playing a role in the U.S. policy of containing China, the United States certainly is interested in exploring this option as reflected in recent moves such as a limited joint military maneuver in 2002. Beside this strategic interest, the large and growing Indian market definitely tempts the Americans in search of new markets. Beside its importance for the American economy, having access to that market will help them reach a strategic interest (i.e., preventing the re-rise of Russia as a fully-fledged superpower). Among other means, this could be achieved through prolonging the process of economic transition of Russia by denying that country its important ally, India, and its large market accustomed to Russian products. Moreover, while India and Pakistan both ignored the United States to declare themselves as nuclear states in May 1998 when they conducted nuclear tests, the U.S. government has been more tolerant about the Indian nuclear program than that of Pakistan. For a variety of reasons, including its lack of a long-range missile or aircraft capability and its very limited financial resources, Pakistan will not be able to pose a serious nuclear threat to the United States for a predictably very long period of time, if ever at all. However, the existence of various extremist groups, including Islamic fundamentalist ones, in Pakistan, the volatility of its political system, and its neighboring unstable Afghanistan still housing terrorist groups should make the U.S. government more concerned about the Pakistani nuclear arsenal than the Indian one. The possibility of its falling in the wrong hands is probably the main source of this concern. As suggested by some Americans in November 2002, a possible Pakistani transfer of nuclear technology to North Korea for its nuclear-weapon project should have aggravated this concern.

The process of polarization in South and West Asia will likely continue as it started earlier in late 2001 unless major political developments change their existing political makeup. In this regard, the most probable event could be a change in the Iranian political system to turn it into a secular state. This seems to be an inevitable scenario in the future due to the depth of dissatisfaction with the existing religious regime among the Iranians and the rapid expansion of dissent all over the country in late 2002. In June 2003 the anti-regime student demonstration in Tehran and many other major cities indicated the possibility of domestically-driven regime change in the near future. During those protests, the students clearly demanded a secular democracy in the place of the ruling theocracy. Taking a violent or peaceful gradual transition, depending on the reaction of the ruling elite to the popular demand for change, a regime change in Iran will help end its isolation. By changing the existing overall political and social situation and by removing the existing barriers to the expansion and development of the Iranian economy and to the active participation of many educated Iranians in their country's affairs, a future secular regime will also release its currently suppressed potential for growth.

However, this major development with a deep impact not only on West and South Asia, but also on other regions such as the Middle East, will not necessarily weaken Iran's commitment to extensive ties, collaboration, and peaceful relations with Russia, India, and China. Its end of isolation, even if it includes a rapprochement with the United States, will only address some of its grievances with the existing international system. For a predictably long period of time until the Iranians address their underdevelopment in various fields and establish themselves as a fully-fledged strong regional power, Iran, under any realistically imaginable form of political system, will remain a dissatisfied state with strong reasons to align itself with other major like-minded countries such as India, China, and Russia. Hence, in the short run, while fluctuations in its ties with the latter are quite probable, Iran will remain in their explicit or implicit grouping or camp.

Having said that, in the long run, this camp with its current membership may not stay together in an explicit or implicit form. As for Iran and Russia, their current pattern of friendship and cooperation is atypical of their relations since the fifteenth century when Russia began to expand southward. In the long run, both Iran and Russia will probably find conflicting interests in certain strategic regions once one of them feels strong enough to pursue its national interests without fear of facing a predictable hostile reaction by the other one. The two will surely find reasons for conflict most probably over political and economic interests in their neighboring Central Asia and the Caucasus to which they have natural ties and where both have strategic interests. Apart from the conflicts over political and economic interests in the countries of those regions, a major source of collision of interests in their bilateral relations will be the issues pertaining to the division of the Caspian Sea and the development of its resources, including but not exclusively, its oil and gas reserves. Moreover, the Iranian or Russian success in dealing with their current problems and their regaining self-confidence may put the two countries on a hostile path. Thus, Iran's success in revitalizing and expanding its economy and the further advancement of its military industry especially in the field of weapons capable of projecting one's power beyond its borders (e.g., medium- and long-range missiles and aircraft) will likely raise concern in its neighboring Russia. In the eyes of the Russians, fear of a rising power along their southern border will change Iran's status from a strategic friend into a potential security threat. Likewise, Russia's ability to solve its various deficiencies and regain a major part or all of its Soviet-era power may incline it to pursue its regional interests more aggressively. The inevitable translation of such an attitude into a high-handed foreign policy toward Iran will make the Iranians fearful of their current friend. In both cases, the result will be an end to their current alliance to be followed by a period of mistrust and hostility.

As for India, its ties with Iran and Russia will not probably deteriorate even in the foreseeable long run. Lacking common borders with the mentioned states, India is and will be immune to many conflicts arising usually in the bilateral relations of neighbors. Its interest in the regions of importance to the other two states is not extensive enough to create major conflicts. In particular, its interest in Central Asia, the Caucasus, and Afghanistan is welcomed by Iran and Russia as it slows down the expansion of both Pakistan and the United States there. Lacking a direct land link with those regions, India's dependency on Iran to access them will create practical limits on its scale of involvement in Central Asia and the Caucasus. To this, one should add other barriers to its rapid growth in those markets, such as its limited marketable products and investment capabilities. As a result, a major clash of interests between India and Iran or Russia will be a highly unlikely scenario in the foreseeable future, at least so long as it has not resolved its various economic problems creating natural limits on its political and economic abilities abroad. Additionally, both Iran and Russia have a variety of long-term incentives to avoid conflicts with India, including their interest in keeping Pakistan in check, in preventing India's forging a strategic alliance with the United States, and in accessing its large and growing market of importance to the economic progress of the two states.

As for China, its ties with Iran will most probably remain friendly for a predictably long time. Lacking a history of conflict and animosity, the absence of any major reason for conflict at the present time and in the foreseeable future will eliminate the possibility of sudden upheavals in their bilateral relations. China's growing economic ties with its neighboring Kazakhstan and Kyrgyzstan are not developing in a manner to jeopardize Iran's long-term interests in Central Asia. Contrary to its ties with Iran, China's relations with India and Russia will probably experience difficulties given their history of conflict. However, such a scenario is not likely to happen in the short term. This is an outcome of a lack of interest in the three states in engaging themselves in major conflicts with their neighbors and their need for a long period of peace to deal with their various economic deficiencies and underdevelopment. In the long run, one should expect the emergence of conflicts in China's ties with India and Russia once the Chinese feel confident enough to seek their interests aggressively or to take an opportunity to settle scores. Being the humiliated side in Chinese-Indian relations, it is more likely that, in the future, India will seek confrontation with China, and not vice versa. As for Russian-Chinese relations, given the benefits of Chinese-Russian economic relations for both sides, neither side should have a major incentive to provoke conflicts or escalate the existing ones in the near future. Furthermore, neither side should have a major reason for confrontation so long as its economic problems persist. Currently, there is not a major source of conflict in their bilateral relations, which could develop into a serious conflict. However, as the growth engine of the twenty-first century, the two countries' interest in Asia and the Pacific region where both wish to expand will likely put them on a hostile path. At that juncture, the reemergence of the old pattern of mistrust will revive their unresolved old grievances to contribute to the escalation of their conflicts. Russia's growing economic interest in the Pacific region, in particular, as reflected in its recent efforts to penetrate its military market, suggests the feasibly of this collision scenario in the future once one side feels strong enough to challenge the other side.

For various reasons, Iran has the opportunity to keep all its options open. Because of its historical friendly ties with China and for its fear of isolation, it could, and there is every indication that it will, continue its friendly ties with China regardless of any future fluctuation in the latter's ties with India or Russia. As well, it will likely continue and expand its growing relations with the European Union (EU). This will be justified for its own merits and also as a means to offset the pressure of the United States and to ensure Russia's inability to squeeze Iran for concessions by threatening to tilt toward the EU should the Russians opt to do so. Moreover, Iran under a future secular regime will probably seek to improve its ties with the United

States, if it can ensure the feasibility of establishing a type of relations with that country different from those of the Shah era. In such relations, Iran is treated as an equal. As well, it allows Iran to preserve its independence, sovereignty, and territorial integrity, while respecting Iranian regional interests. The overall direction of the American government's foreign policy will determine whether the American side will be interested in such relations. However, even if the Iranian-desired relations are established, Iran will likely continue its cooperation with the other three dissatisfied regional powers. Overreliance on the United States, as was the case before the 1979 revolution, would be a non-option, given major changes in Iranian society and the Iranians' lack of interest in accepting a role and a position in international affairs lower than that of a regional power.

The creation of the two rival camps will have a major impact on the regional system in South and West Asia. The efforts of each camp to expand its political, economic, and military presence in major arenas of their rivalry, namely Afghanistan, Central Asia, the Caucasus, and the Persian Gulf, will certainly put them on a path of collision. The specifics of any given situation and the importance of an interest at stake will determine the exact form of such collision of interests. Each camp will seek to have the regional countries on its side with a result of a fierce competition between the two camps, as groups or individuals. This situation will enable the regional countries to maximize their gains by giving them a bargaining chip. In Central Asia and the Caucasus, the main target of rivalry will be the oil/gas-producing countries (Kazakhstan, Turkmenistan, and Azerbaijan) for the importance of their energy resources, for their potential richness and strong financial capability, and for their more prosperous population creating a potentially more lucrative market compared to other regional countries.

In particular, major conflicts will likely arise between the two camps, and especially between Iran and Russia on one side, and America and Pakistan, on the other side, over the issue of oil/gas exports from the Caspian region. Aimed at bypassing Iran and Russia, the beginning of construction of the Baku-Tiblisi-Ceyhan oil pipeline project in September 2002 made the latter angry as the losing side. This is notwithstanding the possibilities that the project may never be completed or, if it is, may not be economically viable. Any major efforts to export oil and gas via the Pakistani route through Afghanistan surely will provoke serious conflicts and could eliminate Iran and Russia from Caspian export projects, an unacceptable scenario for the two countries.

Apart from the oil and gas producers, other regional countries may also be a target of rivalry for noneconomic reasons. The reasons include a potential role they could play in containing, in keeping in check, or in putting pressure on certain regional countries by one camp or another. This potential stems from their sharing borders with certain countries and/or from having natural links (e.g., ethnic, linguistic, and economic) with those countries.

Consequently, the regional countries could become important for the opportunity they offer to one camp or another to affect the pace of events in China (Kazakhstan, Kyrgyzstan, and Tajikistan), in Russia (Kazakhstan, Azerbaijan, and Georgia), in Iran (Azerbaijan, Armenia, and Turkmenistan), and in Afghanistan (Iran, China, Pakistan, Tajikistan, Uzbekistan, and Turkmenistan).

In the Persian Gulf region, Iran, Russia, and China will likely seek to expand and to limit the massive American military, economic, and political presence. The growing anti-American sentiment in that region both within their population and their elites will be a major positive point for the three countries to capitalize on in their bid to expand their relations with the Persian Gulf Arab countries. If the current trend continues, Iran will be a major winner in this region along which it shares a border. Its ties with all the southern Persian Gulf countries have been growing since 1997 to include diplomatic, political, economic and, increasingly so, military/security relations. In particular, Saudi Arabia and Kuwait have been the two most eager countries in expanding relations with Iran. A future secular Iranian government will surely find a lot more opportunity for better ties and extensive relations with its southern neighbors. In particular, those rich states will find a stronger incentive to invest in the Iranian economy. Their fear of the confiscation of their legitimate bank accounts or investments in the United States and, to a lesser extent, in Europe, for a suspicion of a possible link with al-Qaeda or because of a sudden deterioration of their relations with the United States, have led to their extensive transfer of funds from there to safer places since 11 September 2001. So far, Iran has received a small portion of this transaction, but it should receive more once it has a secular regime with a more reliable and predictable nature.

The competition between the two camps will have a significant impact on the international system. While Iran, India, Russia, and China have sought to consolidate the emerging multipolar system of the post–Cold War era, the United States has strived to establish an American-led unipolar system. The success of the former in their rivalry with the United States will play a strong role in the consolidation of their desired system, an objective also supported by the EU. This regional organization has been seeking to establish itself as a powerful pole, which is feasible only in a multipolar system. Given the importance of energy resources of the Persian Gulf and the Caspian Sea regions and their respective lucrative or potentially lucrative markets, the domination of one camp over those regions or its securing a strong and solid position there will surely determine, as a major factor, which side will have a chance to create its desired system.

Thus, efforts to dominate one of these oil-producing and rich regions and exclude the rival camp will provoke a significant reaction by the other side, including a possible military confrontation. The massive and growing presence of the American military in those regions will increase the possibility of such confrontation. As well, any American effort to complete the encirclement of Iran or Russia through further deployment of troops in the Central Asian and Caucasian countries with no American military presence will most probably provoke hostility with a more likely possibility for a military confrontation. In particular, the creation of a pro-American Iraqi regime, now an achievable objective for the Americans as they occupy Iraq, will surely provoke an Iranian reaction, which may take a military form of some sort under certain circumstances. In all imaginable cases, the overall regional and international atmosphere and the ability of each side of the conflict at a given time will determine the scale, length, and significance of any military confrontation. Having said this, there is no inevitability in these scenarios. Taking into consideration the destructive political and material impact of a major military engagement for all the regional and non-regional parties to such a case, intentional efforts on both sides to any given case of conflicting interest and the efforts by regional and international organizations could well prevent the catastrophic results of a twenty-first century war in the strategically important regions of the Persian Gulf and the Caspian Sea.

Bibliography

BOOKS

Brentjes, Burchard and Helga Brentjes. *Taliban: A Shadow Over Afghanistan.* Varanasi, India: Rishi Publications, 2002.

Clubb, O. Edmund. *20th Century China,* 3rd edition. New York: Columbia University Press, 1978.

Hosking, Geoffrey. *A History of the Soviet Union.* London: Fontana Paperbacks and William Collins, 1985.

Marantz, Paul. *From Lenin to Gorbachev: Changing Soviet Perspectives on East-West Relations.* Ottawa: Canadian Institute for International Peace and Security, May 1988.

Maxwell, Ned. *India's China War.* London: Jonathan Cape, 1971.

Moshaver, Ziba. *Nuclear Weapons Proliferation in the Indian Subcontinent.* New York: St. Martin's Press, 1991.

Nojumi, Neamatollah. *The Rise of the Taliban in Afghanistan: Mass Mobilization, Civil War, and the Future of the Region.* London: Palgrave Macmillan, 2001.

Peimani, Hooman. *The Caspian Pipeline Dilemma: Political Games and Economic Losses.* Westport, CT: Praeger, 2001.

———. *Failed Transition, Bleak Future? War and Instability in Central Asia and the Caucasus.* Westport, CT: Praeger, 2002.

———. *Iran and the United States: The Rise of the West Asian Regional Grouping.* Westport, CT: Praeger, 1999.

———. *Nuclear Proliferation in the Indian Subcontinent: The Self-Exhausting "Superpowers" and Emerging Alliances.* Westport, CT: Praeger, 2000.

———. *Regional Security and the Future of Central Asia: The Competition of Iran, Turkey, and Russia.* Westport, CT: Praeger, 1998.

Rashid, Ahmed. *Taliban: Islam, Oil and the New Great Game in Central Asia.* London: I. B. Tauris, May 2002.

Rizvi, H. *The Military and Politics in Pakistan.* Lahore: Progressive Publishers, 1974.

Saddiqui, Karim. *Conflict, Crisis, and War in Pakistan.* Lahore: Macmillan, 1972.

Saliq, S. *Witness to Surrender.* Karachi: Oxford University Press, 1978.

Singh, Maj. Gen. Sukhwant. *India's War Since Independence.* New Delhi: Lancer, 1986.

JOURNAL ARTICLES

Amirahmadian, Bahram. "The Trend of Developments in the Karabakh Crisis." *Majelieh-e Motaellat-e Asyaie Markazi va Ghafghaz* [Central Asia and the Caucasus Review] (Tehran), 28 (Winter 2000), 27–50.

Clark, Kate. "Simmering Feuds." *Middle East International,* 16 August 2002, 22.

"Iran's New Agreements on Energy." *Eurasian File* (Ankara) 112 (January 1999), 7.

Jamestown Foundation. *Monitor* 8, no. 76, 18 April 2002. (Internet version)

"July Chronology." *Middle East International* 482 (26 August 1994), 15.

"Kazakhstan and Russia Sign Agreement on Oil Transit," 7, no. 13, 27 June 2002. (Internet version)

Kazi, Aftab and Tariq Saeedi. "India and the Politics of the Trans-Afghan Gas Pipeline." *Central Asia—Caucasus Analyst* (Baltimore), 28 August 2002. (Internet version)

"Kyrygzstan Political Crisis." International Crisis Group Media Release (Osh/Brussels), 20 August 2002. (Internet version)

Lelyveld, Michael. "Caspian: U.S. Says Patrol Boats Are Gifts to Promote Regional Security." *REF/RL,* 26 June 2001.

Misra, Amalendu. "India at 50: Democracy, Nationalism and Foreign Policy Choices." *Asian Affairs* 30, part 1 (February 1999), 45–58.

Peimani, Hooman. "Afghanistan-Based International Drug-Trafficking: A Continued Threat." *Central Asia-Caucasus Analyst* (Baltimore), 8 May 2002. (Internet version)

Shafaq, Mohammad Nasser and Habiburahmah Ibrahimi. *ISAF Promises Crackdown on Saboteurs.* Institute of War and Peace Reporting. 20 January 2003.

"Turkey Anti-Terrorism Agreement with Iran." *Keesing's Record of World Events* 39, no. 12 (December 1993), 39790.

Zaman, Amberin. "Turkey: A Polarized Society." *The Middle East* 222 (April 1993), 25.

MAGAZINE ARTICLES

"Guard Tries to Kill President." *Guardian* (unlimited), 5 September 2002. (Internet version)

"Intelligence: Explosive Mission." *Far Eastern Economic Review,* 1 April 1999, 6.

Regional Briefing: Afghanistan." *Far Eastern Economic Review,* 26 September 2002, 12.

"Warlords Huddle with Hekmatyar." *Far Eastern Economic Review,* 26 September 2002, 8.

"The World This Week." *The Economist,* 31 August 2002, 6.

NEWSPAPER ARTICLES

"An American Expert: The USA Has No Choice but to Remove Sanction Against Iran." *Ettela'at Binolmelali* (Tehran), 30 April 1998, 1.

"Airbus Sale Fell Through." *Iran* (Tehran), 1 October 2002, 1.

"Australia Voices Readiness to Invest in Iran Oil Projects." *Ettela'at Binolmelali* (Tehran), 26 May 1998, 12.

Brooke, James. "Putin Greets North Korean Leader on Russia's Pacific Coast." *The New York Times,* 24 August 2002. (Internet version)

Devraj, Ranjit. "China Behind Pakistan's Missile Tests, Says India." *Asia Time online* (Hong Kong), 8 October 2002. (Internet version)

"Dr. Rohani: Afghanistan Will Not Become Pakistan's Backyard." *Ettela'at Binolmelali* (Tehran), 17 August 1998, 6.

"Drug Addiction Devastates the Youth." *Abrar* (Tehran), 15 July 2002, 6.

Eckholm, Eril. "American Gives Beijing Good News: Rebels on Terror List." *The New York Times,* 26 August 2002. (Internet version)

"Illegal Migration of Afghans to Iran Has Resumed." *Ettela'at Binolmelali* (Tehran), 8 August 2002, 2.

"Iranian President Condemns Assassination Attempt on President Karzai." *Ettela'at Binolmelali* (Tehran), 9 August 2002, 2.

"Iranian Representative: We Spend 400 Million Dollars Annually to Combat Drug-Trafficking." *Ettela'at Binolmelali* (Tehran), 16 March 1998, 2.

Maitra, Ramtanu. "Indian Military Showdown over Central Asia." *Asia Times online* (Hong Kong), 10 September 2002. (Internet version)

Meyers, Steven Lee. "Russia Recasts Bog in Caucasus as War on Terror." *The New York Times,* 2 October 2002. (Internet version)

"MJF Plans to Invest $3 Billion in Gas Pipeline to Pakistan." *Ettela'at Binolmelali* (Tehran), 5 February 1998, 12.

"Nato Strikes Deal to Accept Russia in a Partnership." *The New York Times,* 15 May 2002. (Internet version)

"Opinion Poll Results Indicate Dissatisfaction." *Ettela'at* (Tehran), 21 October 2002, 4.

"Pakistan Stuns Airbus, Opt for Boeing." *Asia Times online* (Hong Kong), 28 August 2002. (Internet version)

"Pipeline to Transfer Turkmen Gas Via Iran Became Operational." *Ettela'at Binolmelali* (Tehran), 5 January 1998, 12.

Peimani, Hooman. "Bahrain Turns to Iran." *Asia Times online* (Hong Kong), 22 August 2002. (Internet version)

———. "Drug-Trafficking in the Ferghana Valley and Instability in Central Asia." *The Times of Central Asia* (Bishkek), 2 November 2002, 4. (Internet version)

———. "Eurasian Transport Link Faces Roadblocks." *Asia Times online* (Hong Kong), 14 June 2002. (Internet version)

———. "Iran and Kuwait Close Ranks." *Asia Times online* (Hong Kong), 25 September 2002. (Internet version)

———. "Military Buidup Ends US-Russian Honeymoon." *Asia Times online* (Hong Kong), 29 August 2002.

———. "The Ties That Bind Iran and Saudi Arabia." *Asia Times online* (Hong Kong), 16 August 2002. (Internet version)

"Project for the Transfer of Gas of the South Pars Field to India and Pakistan Will Begin." *Abrar* (Tehran), 9 April 1998, 4.

Ramachandran, Sudha. "India, Iran, Russia Map Out Trade Route." *Asia Times online* (Hong Kong), 29 June 2002. (Internet version)

"Released Opinion Poll Results Provoke Harsh Reactions." *Ettela'at* (Tehran), 24 October 2002, 4.

Rosenthal, Elisabeth. "China Seems to Deny Pakistan a Nuclear Umbrella." *The New York Times,* 21 May 1998. (Internet version)

Shanker, Thom with John F. Burns. "State Department to Take Over Security for Afghan Leader." *The New York Times,* 25 August 2002. (Internet version)

"Student Protests Held at Tehran Campuses." *Abrar* (Tehran), 18 November 2002, 2.

"We Will Not Repeat the Mistake We Made with the Afghan Refugees." *Ettela'at Binolmelali,* 7 August 2002, 2.

"Zangene: We Resolved Our Export Problem." *Hamsahrye* (Tehran), 10 October 2002, 2.

OTHER SOURCES

Babaev, Joldas. "Kazak Journalists Face Brutal Intimidation Unidentified 'Hooligans' Wage Reign of Terror on Opposition Journalists." From: "kevmille," kevmille@indiana.edu, *Central Asia News,* 30 May 2002, 06:58:36-0000. (Internet publication)

"China: Xinjiang Uighur Autonomous Region." *Amnesty International Report 2002.* (Internet version)

Drug Abuse Prevention, Republic of Belarus. info@nodrug.by.www.correspondent.net, July 28, 2001.

FAO/WFP. Crop and Food Supply Assessment for 2002/2003, 16 August 2002.

The Global Development Briefing, 17 October 2002. (Internet publication)

———. 10 October 2002.

———. 26 September 2002.

———. 19 September 2002.

———. 12 September 2002.

Miller, Jr., Kevin. "Afghanistan: UN Optimistic after Government Moves on Opium." kevmille@indiana.edu, *Central Asia News,* 5 April 2002, 22:23:48-0500. (Internet publication)

News. BBC World, 14 November 2002.

News. Radio of the Islamic Republic of Iran, 14 October 2002.

Population Division and Statistics of the United Nations Secretariat, 2002. (Internet version)

RFE/RL. 12 November 2002.

———. 7 October 2002.

———. 24 August 2002.

"Russia, China Sign Friendship Treaty." *Associated Press,* 16 July 2001.

Text: President Putin's State of the Nation Address, unofficial translation of full text by Vladimir Vladimirovich Putin. The Russian Observer, Observer.com. Issued on 04.18.2002 (MST).

"Turkey." Eia Country Analysis Brief, July 2002 (eia-doe.gov).

UNDP. *Human Development Report 2001*. New York: Oxford University Press, 2001.

United Nations High Commissioner for Refugees (UNHCR), 10 September 2002.

UNSCN. "Asia—Selected Situations: Afghanistan Region." *RNIS* 39, October 2002, 47.

"U.S. Concern: Moscow-Beijing Arms Deals." United Press International (UPI), 30 November 2000. (Accessed via NewsMax.com Wires)

WHO-UNICEF. Statistics. 2002. (Internet version)

Woodrow, Thomas. "China Rising, America Sleeping." The Jamestown Foundation, 1 August 2002, republished by Information, info@mail.uyghurinfo.com, in *Central Asia News*, 2 August 2002, 12:03:55-0700 (PDT).

The World Bank. Quoted in Afghanistan-Country Report, Jane's Information Group, June 2003. (Internet version)

———. Statistics. 17 April 2003. (Internet version)

———. *World Development Indicators 2001*. Washington, D.C.: The World Bank, 2001.

2001 National Trade Estimate Report on Foreign Trade Barriers, United States Department of Trade, website.

Index

About the Author

HOOMAN PEIMANI works as an independent consultant with international organizations in Geneva, Switzerland, and does research in international relations. His writing has centered on the Persian Gulf, the Caucasus, Central Asia, and the Indian subcontinent. Apart from various journal and newspaper articles, his recent publications include *Failed Transition, Bleak Future? War and Instability in Central Asia and the Caucasus* (Praeger, 2002); *The Caspian Pipeline Dilemma: Political Games and Economic Losses* (Praeger, 2001); *Nuclear Proliferation in the Indian Subcontinent: The Self-Exhausting "Superpowers" and Emerging Alliances* (Praeger, 2000); *Iran and the United States: The Rise of the West Asian Regional Grouping* (Praeger, 1999); and *Regional Security and the Future of Central Asia: The Competition of Iran, Turkey, and Russia* (Praeger, 1998).